MORGELLONS AND RED MERCURY "PLAGUES" CREATED IN THE NWO LABS OF "MAD SCIENTISTS"

The Final Nail . . .
IN YOUR COFFIN!
A POX TO ALL OF MANKIND

Commander X - Sean Casteel And Tim R. Swartz

The Final Nail In Your Coffin!

A POX TO ALL OF MANKIND

Inner Light/Global Communications

The Final Nail...In Your Coffin! - A Pox To All Of Mankind
By Commander X, Sean Casteel and Tim R. Swartz

Printed in the United States of America

Inner Light/Global Communications, P.O. Box 753,
New Brunswick, NJ 08903

Please address any questions about this book to:
mrufo8@hotmail.com

Timothy Green Beckley: Editorial Director
Carol Ann Rodriguez: Publishers Assistant
Tim R. Swartz: Editor
Sean Casteel: Associate Editor
William Kern: Associate Editor
Cover Graphics: Prometeus,
Dreamstime.com - Halloween Simbol Photo

For Free Subscription To The Conspiracy Journal Write:
Tim Beckley/Global Communications
Box 753, New Brunswick, NJ 08903

Email: mrufo8@hotmail.com

www.ConspiracyJournal.Com

www.TeslasSecretLab.Com

CONTENTS

Folksinger Joni Mitchell Battles Morgellons 7

1. The Fiber Disease 23

2. The Biowarfare Conspiracy 35

3. Was Morgellons Developed in A Lab?..53

4. Is Morgellons From Outer Space? 62

5. All in Their Heads 75

SECTION TWO - RED MERCURY

6. Nuclear Secrets 85

7. Red Mercury: Fact or Fiction? 96

8. Seeds of Destruction: Bioterrorism 106

9. A Conspiracy to Spread Disease and Death 119

10. How Safe Is Our Food Supply?..126

11. Nostradamus Predictions of World War Three 133

12. Aum Shinrikyo's Search for Tesla Technology 135

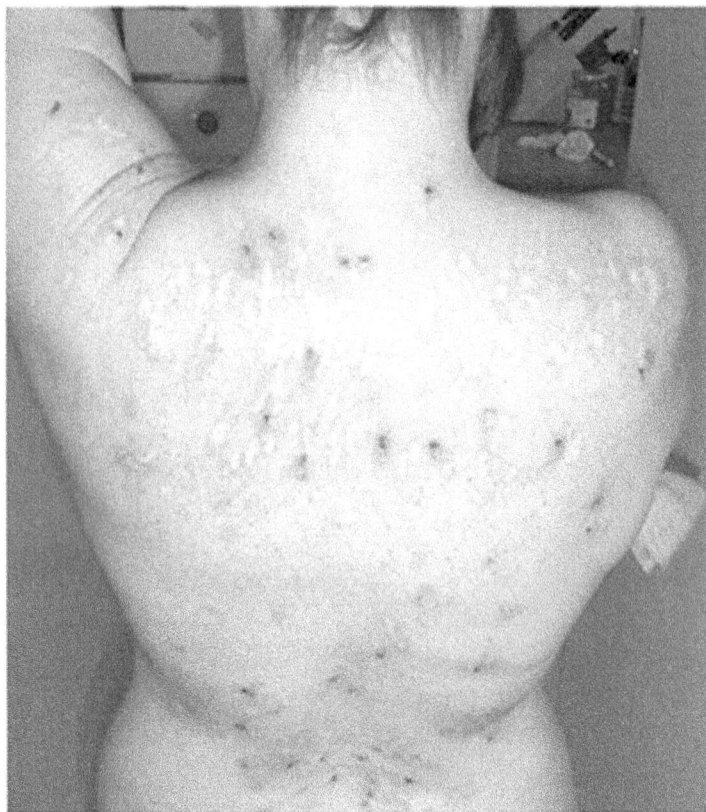

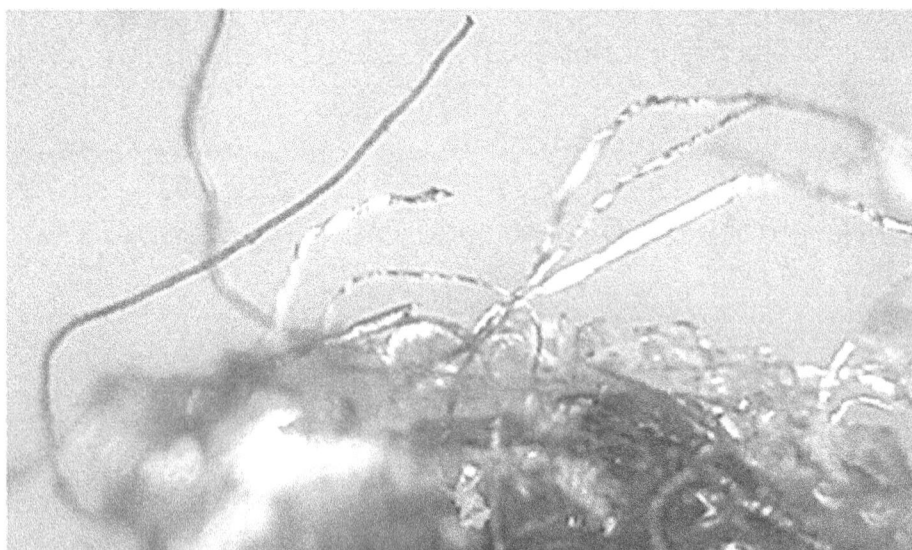

Morgellons sufferers often experience relentless itching, skin sores that do not heal, and even more mystifying, strange fibers that grow out of their skin.

FOLKSINGER JONI MITCHELL BATTLES MORGELLONS –
"SEEMS LIKE IT'S FROM OUTER SPACE!"
By Sean Casteel

ON a Tuesday evening, March 31, 2015, the legendary folk singer Joni Mitchell was hospitalized after being found unconscious in her Los Angeles home. It was unclear what had caused her to pass out, but Mitchell, who was 71 at the time of her hospitalization, had long identified herself as a sufferer of the strange and controversial condition called Morgellons Disease.

Mitchell told "*The Los Angeles Times*" in a 2010 interview that Morgellons Disease "seems like it's from outer space." In her 2014 autobiography, entitled "*Joni Mitchell: In Her Own Words*," she writes, "I couldn't wear clothing. I couldn't leave my house for several years. Sometimes it got so I'd have to crawl across the floor. My legs would cramp up, just like a polio spasm. It hit all of the places where I had polio."

A QUICK BIO OF JONI MITCHELL

For those born after the counterculture began to flourish in the 1960s, it might be helpful to talk a little about Joni Mitchell's life. She was born Roberta Joan Anderson on November 7, 1943, in Fort Macleod, Canada. She contracted polio at the age of nine, and it was during her recovery in the hospital that she began performing and singing to her fellow patients. After teaching herself to play guitar, she quickly emerged as one of the leading folk performers of the late 1960s and 1970s. Her unique guitar tunings were created to compensate for the polio of her childhood, which left her unable to use the fret fingering patterns for standard tuning.

Mitchell's original songs were distinctive and highly personal in their lyrical imagery and drew the attention of folk music audiences in Toronto even in her teens. She married American folksinger Chuck Mitchell in 1965 and took his surname. Their short marriage ended in divorce in 1967. She moved to the U.S. and recorded her first album, called "Joni Mitchell," in 1968, with David Crosby handling the production chores. Other successful albums followed. Mitchell won her first Grammy Award – for Best Folk Performance – in 1969 with her second album, "Clouds." She achieved mainstream success with "Ladies of the Canyon," her third album, which included the hits "Circle Game" and "Big Yellow Taxi."

Her biggest commercial success was 1974's "Court and Spark," a foray into jazz and jazz fusion music. The album was nominated for four Grammy awards and spawned the hits "Help Me" and "Free Man In Paris." Over the years, Mitchell continued to garner Grammy nominations in various categories. She was inducted into the Rock and Roll Hall of Fame in 1997 and the Canadian Songwriters Hall of Fame in 2007. Her songs became hits for other performers as well, including Judy Collins, the Counting Crows and Crosby, Stills, Nash and Young, the latter making a smash success out of Mitchell's song, "Woodstock," in 1970. Mitchell did not attend that legendary music festival herself but based the song on reports she received from friends who had. Mitchell has been called the best female songwriter of the modern, post-World War II era of popular music and her influence on other writers and performers has been enormous.

She told *"Rolling Stone"* in 2002 that she was retiring due to her frustration with the music industry, which she called a "cesspool." However, she continued to issue various compilation albums of her earlier work and in 2007 released "Shine," her first album of new songs in almost a decade. The album was politically charged and environmentally conscious and charted well on the Billboard 200 list, both debuting and peaking at number 14 in spite of Mitchell's long absence from the music scene.

Joni Mitchell

Mitchell says her singing voice has faltered in recent years due to complications from her childhood polio and a compressed larynx and denies that her lifelong smoking is the true cause. She no longer tours or gives concerts and now invests her time advocating for victims of Morgellons Disease as well as speaking on environmental issues and creating visual art.

WHAT IS JONI MITCHELL'S BIZARRE MALADY?

Just what is Joni Mitchell's bizarre malady, Morgellons Disease? The condition has also been labeled Mitchell's "Secret Torment" by one British newspaper, although she has never made any effort to keep her condition hidden. Quite the opposite, in fact. But talking publicly about Morgellons is not an easy task, especially when the medical establishment refuses for the most part to believe the problem is even a physical "disease" at all.

According to researcher, writer and radio host Tim R. Swartz, who has studied Morgellons for the last several years, "Those with the disease describe feelings of insects scurrying beneath their skin and have mysterious sores that ooze out blue and white fibers, some as thick as spaghetti strands. Attempts to remove the fibers are said to produce shooting pains radiating from the site." Sufferers may also report fatigue and problems with short-term memory and concentration.

Morgellons takes its name from the efforts of Mary Leitao, who in 2001 was a 43-year-old stay-at-home Mom and former lab technician in South Carolina. She noticed that Drew, her two-year-old son, had begun to develop lesions on the inside of his lip that didn't look like typical canker sores. Even more troubling, when she asked him what was wrong, he pointed at his lips and said, "Bugs."

According to Jessica Roy, writing in an online publication called "The Cut": "Leitao used a toy microscope, purchased at Radio Shack for $8, to investigate Drew's sores, and found what looked like fibers of various colors growing out of his skin. Alarmed, she took her toddler to a doctor near her home, followed by several others. None of them could say for sure what was causing the lesions because none of them could find anything biologically wrong with Drew." In fact, some of the doctors concluded that Mary Leitao herself suffered from "Munchausen by proxy," a psychological condition where people seek attention for an invented illness, and that her son wasn't actually sick.

Dr. Fred Heldrich, a specialist in medical mystery cases at Johns Hopkins, examined Drew. "I found no evidence of anything suspicious in Andrew," Heldrich wrote to the physician who had referred the young boy to him. "Ms. Leitao would benefit from a psychiatric evaluation and support, whether Andrew has Morgellons Disease or not. I hope she will cease to use her son in further exploring this problem."

It was Leitao who coined her son's ailment as "Morgellons," named after a medical condition described in 1674 by the British author Thomas Browne. Browne said the disorder caused children to "critically break out with harsh hairs on their backs," though even the Morgellons Research Foundation says it is doubtful that the 17th century disease is related in any way to modern day Morgellons, writes Swartz.

Having failed to have Drew's condition recognized by the medical community, Leitao pressed on. Her efforts both online and off instigated a rash of Morgellons self-diagnoses that many now chalk up to a unique type of Internet-proliferated mass hysteria. Leitao launched a website in 2004 where she published her amateur findings about the disease. Drew was her test subject in experiments where she used her biology background to pluck fibers from his wounds and closely study them in the hope that she would connect with others suffering from similar symptoms.

DIAGNOSIS: "DELUSIONAL"

Mary Leitao was not alone in being disappointed by the medical community's bafflement and indifference to her son's condition. After Morgellons Disease became more widely known through her public awareness campaign, thousands of sufferers also encountered much the same response from their doctors.

Dr. Anand Veeravagu, writing on the website "The Daily Beast," explains, "In adults, the disease is more generally referred to as 'delusional parasitosis' (DP). Many patients with Morgellons strongly reject the idea of their condition being seen as a derivative of DP, and believe that it is a poorly understood dermatological condition rather than a psychiatric disturbance. Thus, in many cases, Morgellons is referred to as an 'unexplained dermatopathology.' One of the key distinguishing characteristics between Morgellons and DP is that patients with Morgellons may report an infestation with inanimate objects or strange cloth-like fibers.

"There are two parts to DP," Dr. Veeravagu continues. "The first is delusion. Patients with DP have a very specific delusion, defined as a person's belief that cannot be corrected by reasoning, persuasion or logical argument. The second part is the substance of the delusion. In those with Morgellons, the fixed belief is that the person is infected with 'bugs' such as parasites, bacteria, mites or fibers. Those who have the recurring thought present themselves to primary care doctors and dermatologists with rashes, skin excoriations and wounds. All laboratory tests and pathogenic exams return negative. Patients don't have infections, bugs or other infestations. Many times the mysterious 'fibers' appear to be nothing more than cotton."

Dr. Veeravagu adds that current treatment for the disease varies widely but it is better for patients to pursue psychiatric care to examine the source of the delusion and take the appropriate medication, which often means antidepressants. Patients who reject the notion of a psychiatric cause have often turned to alternative therapies and some even tried veterinary medications designed to rid animals of certain types of infections.

In April, 2006, the Centers for Disease Control recommended an epidemiological investigation of what they were then referring to as a public health concern. In January, 2008, they announced a grant to healthcare giant Kaiser Permanente to test and interview 150 to 500 patients suffering from Morgellons. Kaiser Permanente doctors have been among the most ready to classify Morgellons as delusional parasitosis, and the results of the testing were as expected. No abnormal findings, no swarms of parasites. In its 2012 report, the CDC said that the study found that "no common underlying medical condition or infectious source was identified, similar to more commonly recognized conditions such as delusional infestation." The researchers also concluded the fibers were likely from clothing that got trapped in the patients' sores and were not the cause of the skin irritation.

A similar study by the Mayo Clinic in 2011 had looked at 108 patients with symptoms of Morgellons and the conclusions were the same: no evidence of skin infestation.

Morgellons naysayers believe that the disease is not only a personal delusion suffered by individuals, it has also become a form of "mass delusional hysteria," driven by the Internet, in which people are led to inexpertly diagnose themselves and join a kind of Morgellons "community" of sufferers based on no medical evidence at all. But the continuing stigma of the mental illness diagnosis makes Morgellons patients all the more determined to find a strictly medical cause for their suffering.

IS MORGELLONS A KIND OF BIOWEAPON OF TERROR?

Tim R. Swartz has done some digging into the conspiracy-related aspects of Morgellons, taking it out of the category of "medical anomaly" and placing it squarely in the realm of bioweapons. He begins his argument by explaining that those with the debilitating symptoms of Morgellons are often found to have contracted Lyme disease sometime in their past. Doctors are still trying to determine if there is a biological connection between the two or if Morgellons is simply exploiting an already compromised immune system.

"There have been allegations over the years," Swartz writes, "that Lyme disease was a natural disease made worse by genetic manipulation. The focus of these accusations is a research facility on Plum Island, just off Orient Point, Long Island, and six miles from the Connecticut coast. In 1954, research there was influenced by the Cold War and scientists began studying ways to inflict damage on Soviet livestock. The Cuban government alleges that in the 1960s and 70s, bioweapons developed at Plum Island were deployed against Cuban agriculture, targeting pork, tobacco and sugar cane.

"In surrounding areas," he continues, "distrust of Plum Island runs deep. Lyme disease takes its name from a Connecticut town across from the island; many wonder whether birds or swimming animals could have brought the disease from Plum Island. Some suspect it may have been deliberately released. Others speculate that Morgellons may have also originated on the island. Plum Island officials, of course, dismiss such hypotheses as fantasy."

Swartz refers to Dr. Len Horowitz, America's most controversial medical authority, who charges that elements of the U.S. government are conspiring with major pharmaceutical companies to make large elements of the population sick. More than that, Dr. Horowitz accuses the same conspirators of creating the AIDS epidemic to kill blacks, Hispanics and gays. Morgellons fits very neatly within Dr. Horowitz's disturbing scenario of manmade diseases being secretly released on an unsuspecting population.

Another disturbing possibility offered by Swartz is that Morgellons is caused by nano-machines in the form of "nanofibers," one of the latest trends in computer miniaturization. Fiber samples taken from the skin of a

Morgellons sufferer, when exposed to heat, did not burn until heated to 1700 degrees Fahrenheit. Also, under examination with an electron microscope, fiber samples appear to be nonorganic. They have no eukaryotic cells and no cell membrane. Meaning that Morgellons is not a parasite, is not biological at all, but is a machine.

THE "NANO-MACHINE" THEORY

Under testing by the research unit of Integrative Health International at Lakewood, California, Morgellons appears to be a "communicable nanotechnology invasion of human tissue in the form of self-assembling, self-replicating nanotubes, nanowires and nano-arrays with sensors." Morgellons nano-machines are commonly found in all body fluids, orifices and often even hair follicles, and are believed to routinely achieve total body systemic penetration. They also seem to possess a hive or "group intelligence" and are configured to receive specific microwave, EMF and ELF signals and radio data.

At this point, why this is happening is anyone's guess. But if these findings are correct, and Morgellons is nanotechnology capable of taking over biological systems, the question remains whether or not the devices were deliberately released with the intention of infecting people for some unknown purpose.

But Swartz posits one possible purpose that sounds quite sinister indeed.

"It is almost as if Morgellons," Swartz writes, "is in the process of 'reconstructing' people into an entirely different lifeform; a cyborg-type creature, both biological and machine. As well, the reports that the Morgellons nano-machines are capable of receiving radio signals could indicate that each infected person/system would be able to communicate with other Morgellons sufferers, creating the potential for each person to be like a single brain cell of a larger, artificial intelligence. We could be seeing the beginning of the end of the human race as we know it."

All of which leads Swartz to ask, "Are we facing an invasion by machine intelligence, or is this a twisted attempt by some unknown group or government to achieve the ultimate control of humankind? When one considers the current world situation – terrorist attacks, domestic spying, governments out of control and the suppression of democracy and freedoms guaranteed by our Founding Fathers – it should come as no surprise that someone could stoop to the evil of releasing something like Morgellons upon an 'unsuspecting' planet. Sometimes the smallest thing can cause the biggest problems. We have to take a deeper look, beyond the affliction itself, before we will find the answers."

WHERE IS MARY LEITAO?

The online publication "The Cut" reports on still another mystery of the continuing Morgellons saga: where is Mary Leitao now?

"Though her website – Morgellons.org – still exists," writes Jessica Roy, "the CDC study was a major blow to Leitao and her research, and, shortly after the CDC's findings were published, she shut down her foundation and donated all its findings to Oklahoma State University. Leitao then disappeared totally from the Morgellons community and hasn't been heard from since; emails sent to her Morgellons.org address bounced back and phone calls to numbers assigned to her name went unanswered. One woman who had spent a long time working with Leitao said neither she nor anyone else in the Morgellons community had spoken to her since 2012 and that no one had any idea how to get in touch with her.

"Even if Morgellons has receded from the spotlight since the CDC's damning report," Roy continues, "Mitchell's recent illness has once again highlighted her role as the illness's most famous flag-bearer. 'I'm actually trying to get out of the music business to battle for Morgellons sufferers,' she told the L.A. Times in 2010. 'So they can receive the credibility that's owed to them.' It's a battle they're still fighting – and without Leitao, the crusading mother who sparked an international medical controversy before vanishing into thin air."

Leitao's disappearance may add fuel to the fire Swartz is stoking of conspiracy and the intentional release of a manmade disease into the population either as a biological agent or the tip of some nanotechnology iceberg. But, admittedly, Leitao's possible role in such a scenario would be difficult to pin down. Was she perhaps "taken out" for bringing public attention to what was intended to be a classified "disease-ops" of some kind?

DR. ROGER LEIR AND THE ALIEN HUNTER

At this point, perhaps we should revisit Mitchell's remark about the maddening malady that is Morgellons being "from outer space." Though probably meant flippantly, there is some evidence that we cannot ignore that point to this statement being not so far from the truth.

The late Dr. Roger Leir, a Southern California podiatrist, performed over a dozen alien implant removal surgeries. Beginning in the mid-1990s up until his death in 2014, Leir took the stories of people who claimed to have been abducted by aliens and implanted with tiny pieces of alien "hardware" at face value. After x-raying the part of the body the abductee indicated had been implanted – the miniature devices would show up every time – Leir and his small medical team would brandish a scalpel and remove the miniscule objects.

Laboratory analysis revealed time and time again that the alien implants were covered in a tough membrane that, while it seemed to be organic living tissue, was nearly impossible to slice through with normal surgical tools. The membrane was of great interest to Leir because of the fact that the patient's tissue surrounding the implant suffered no inflammation at all. Leir often said it would be wonderful if human medical science could duplicate the alien non-inflammatory tissue. If we could wrap organs, such as a liver or heart, in the otherworldly material, we could prevent the body's natural tendency to reject transplanted organs. Somehow the aliens have circumvented the rejection problem and are many years ahead of us in terms of medical knowledge.

This idea of alien implants being part of the recipe for Morgellons echoes Swartz's theory that the disease is caused by communicable nanofibers and not a living parasite or any kind of biological agent at all. Some may laugh at the notion of an alien origin for Morgellons, but, when objectively weighing the evidence, including the nonorganic composition of some Morgellons fibers tested under laboratory conditions, it remains a disturbing possibility.

Researcher/author/publisher Timothy Beckley says that, while admittedly not the same, the descriptions of the Morgellons fibers and the alien implants do resemble each other to a degree, and furthermore they share the quality of being "invaders" or "intruders."

"I have seen some of these implants pretty up-close," Beckley says. "They were shown to me on a couple of occasions by the former private investigator, Derrel Sims, who calls himself 'The Alien Hunter' and insists he is the world's leading expert on alien abduction. His more than 38 years of field research has focused on physical evidence and has led to his groundbreaking discoveries regarding alien implants and alien fluorescence.

"As a former military police officer and CIA operative," Beckley continues, "Sims has a unique insight into the alien organization, which he believes functions in ways similar to an intelligence agency. Sims is also a compassionate and skilled therapist and Certified Master Hypnotherapist who has helped hundreds of alien experiencers all over the world come to terms with what they've witnessed. In his book, ***Alien Hunter: Evidence and Truth About Alien Implants,*** you will read numerous case histories of alien implants from the Texan, who for a while worked with Dr. Leir. Sims is said to have the largest collection of alleged alien implants and artifacts in the world, and each has a fascinating story."

According to Beckley, Mr. Sims was deeply moved and inspired by the haunting memory of his own "implantation" at the age of twelve. Upon reaching adulthood, Sims began to collect anything that could be labeled as physical evidence left behind by beings he sees as very negative – accusing them of kidnapping humans and slipping these artifacts or probes under the skin of those whom they abduct so that the aliens can keep tabs on the activities of these selected humans.

Sims maintains that some of these "alien artifacts" were surgically removed and then given to him by patients, while others were expelled naturally from the body. Sims sees implants as a relatively rare phenomenon, perhaps affecting less than 1% of the abductee population. Yet, in 1995, he finally felt the evidence was compelling enough to formally document the removal of these mysterious objects from two of his most promising cases.

Prior to that, in 1994, Sims was invited to speak at an American Medical Association conference at John Muir Medical Center in the California Bay Area. The title of his talk was "The Medical Complications of Alleged Alien Abductions."

In front of an audience of distinguished medical personnel, he made several predictions about what we would find with regards to genuine alien implants:

"This," says Sims, "set off a veritable firestorm of activity within the UFO community. Suddenly, every abductee began to believe they had an alien implant. Claims were made about the phenomenon by others that were inconsistent with the evidence. Unfortunately, some of these misconceptions persist. Since those heady days of 1995, conventional implant technology has emerged, from microchips in the family dog to medical implants to dispense hormones. Still others have put forth claims of nefarious government implants, which has further clouded the issue."

The Predictions:

1.   The objects would not contain human technology.
2.   The tissue surrounding the object would not exhibit inflammation, either chronic or acute.
3.   There would be nerve cells present in parts of the body where they are not naturally occurring.
4.   Besides the metallic objects, we will begin to see a "biological implant," a cluster of brain cells in another part of the body.

Naturally, many of the doctors in attendance told him that these situations would be highly unusual to say the least. The surgeons who performed the 1995 surgeries he arranged said the same thing before they undertook the operations. To everyone's surprise...***Sims' predictions were accurate!***

Two major studies were done on the recovered objects, one by New Mexico Tech University and the other by Los Alamos Labs. The results were intriguing, though not conclusive. Blind testing done at Los Alamos Lab revealed extraterrestrial isotopes such as would be seen in a rare meteor. Additionally, the form of the metals suggested manufacture as opposed to natural origins. When the scientists discovered that the objects had come from a human body, they scrambled to make sense of what they had just put on record!

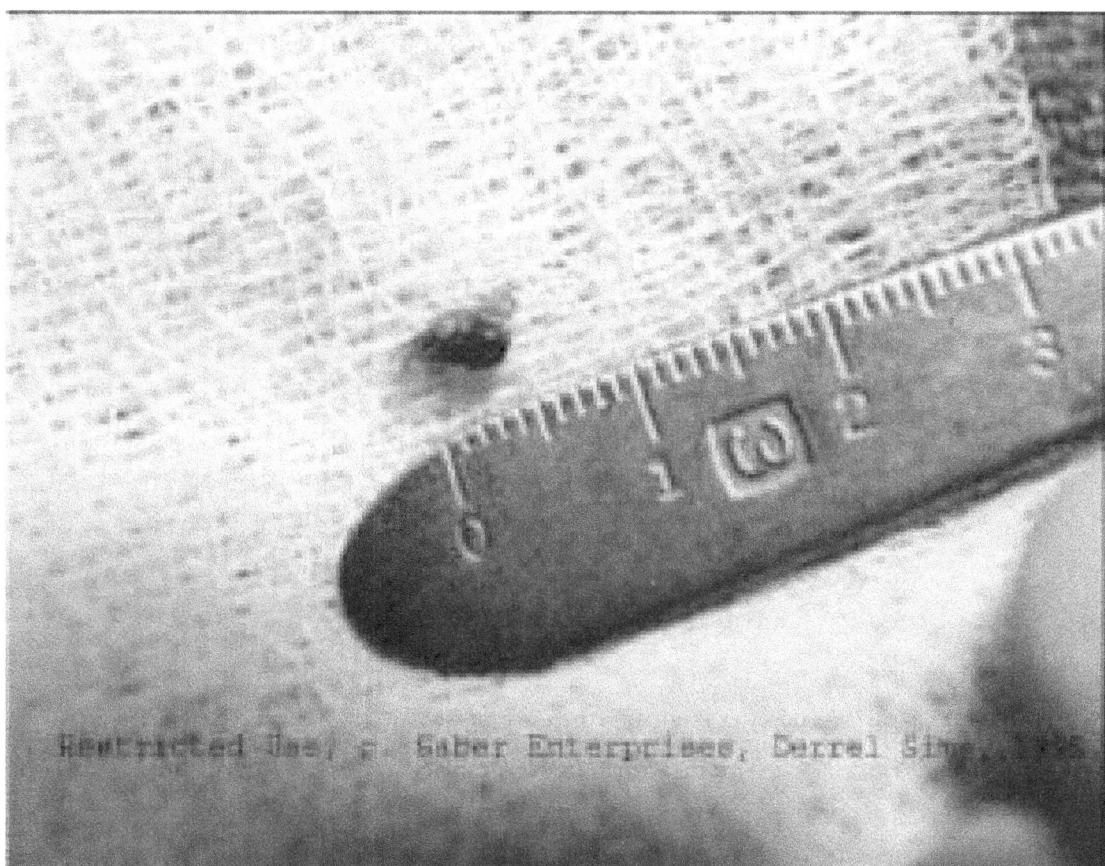

Possible alien implant removed during 1995 public surgeries from one of Derrel Sims' abductees.

Sims' team of medical and scientific consultants continue to study the evidence of alien implants, both in surgically removed objects and anomalous objects still in the body. Much more testing remains to be done, and Sims urges a healthy skepticism while continuing to forge ahead.

One can say the same about Morgellons, which is our main concern here, though we should not turn a blind eye when it comes to alien devices which could ultimately have a significant meaning for those who find their skin crawling with fibers and wire-like objects.

COULD MORGELLONS BE FROM MARS?

Meanwhile, Tim R. Swartz has another provocative theory.

"What makes Morgellons so unique," he writes, "are the weird fibers that grow out of the victim's skin. No other disease on Earth has this bizarre symptom. So could this mean that Morgellons originated somewhere other than Earth?"

Swartz reports on a researcher named Mike Moore who discovered a meteor on a ranch in Texas in the winter of 1970-71. After careful study, Moore concluded that the unusual rock had formed under extremely dry conditions and was volcanic in origin. He believes it came to Earth as a result of the impact of a large asteroid on the surface of Mars.

"When I first found the meteorite," Moore says, "it had just come through our atmosphere, and the outer surface had probably been 'sterilized' by the high heat that melted the entire outer surface of the meteorite. It wasn't until ten or fifteen years later that I noticed that some 'fuzz' or 'filaments' were coming out of the crevice that runs through one side of the meteorite."

Moore was confused about what he was seeing. How could a rock from Mars be growing something that appeared to be alive? It was not until NASA announced in 1996 that they had found the possible remnants of life in a Martian meteorite that Moore began to consider that he was seeing some kind of Martian life growing on his own meteorite.

When he broke off a small sample of the meteorite, "sand" fell out. Using a pocket microscope, he found a piece of something that had obviously come from some kind of plant or at least some living thing. Attached to the small object was a filament. Under the microscope, the filament and the fuzz coming from the crevice were identical, what Moore called "the same creature."

A worker at the Roswell UFO Museum in New Mexico offered to do some tests on the meteorite's contents. Moore gave him a small sample of the sand that had fallen from the middle of the space rock, and the filament creatures were again present in the sample. While trying to glue one end of one of the filaments to a slide for study, the filament moved back and forth, as if trying to avoid being stuck to the slide.

Morgellons patients have also reported a similar movement of the threads and fibers that are associated with their disease. During the alien implant removal surgeries performed by Dr. Leir, the implants would sometimes seem to struggle to avoid the scalpel, moving of their own accord in the abductee's body as if alive and conscious that the operation was happening.

Moore speculates that rocks blown off of Mars have been falling to Earth throughout history, bringing with them the minute lifeforms that we now call Morgellons. What still needs to be answered is whether or not Morgellons adapted itself to Earth conditions millions of years ago or if it is a relatively "new" condition that has surfaced over the last few centuries.

MORPHING MORGELLONS

For her part, Joni Mitchell has said, "Fibers in a variety of colors protrude out of my skin. They cannot be forensically identified as animal, vegetable or mineral. Morgellons is constantly morphing. There are times when it's directly attacking the nervous system, as if you're being bitten by fleas and lice. It's all in the tissue and it's not a hallucination. It was eating me alive, sucking the juices out. I've been sick all my life."

SOURCES FOR THIS CHAPTER

"What is Morgellons? Singer Joni Mitchell's Disputed Diagnosis" by Catherine Saint Louis, "The New York Times," April 1, 2015.

"Inside Morgellons: Joni Mitchell's Mystery Illness," by Dr. Anand Veeravagu, "The Daily Beast," April 1, 2015.

"The Bizarre Backstory of Joni Mitchell's Chronic Illness," by Jessica Roy, "The Cut," April 3, 2015.

"Joni Mitchell suffers from a disease most doctors think isn't real," by Julia Belluz, "Vox," April 2, 2015.

"Joni Mitchell," Biography.com website located at: http://www.biography.com/people/joni-mitchell-9410294

"Morgellons: New Disease or Manmade Terror Weapon?" by Tim R. Swartz, "The Conspiracy Journal Newsletter," http://www.conspiracyjournal.com

"Morgellons: Terrifying New Disease Reaching Pandemic Status," by Barbara Minton, "Natural News," March 3, 2009.

"Could Morgellons Be From Mars?" by Tim R. Swartz, "The Conspiracy Journal Newsletter."

CHAPTER ONE

The Fiber Disease

A mysterious skin disease is currently spreading across the United States, but many doctors are not sure if it is real or just in the heads of the sufferers. It is called Morgellons and the symptoms sound as if they could have been lifted straight from the pages of a science fiction book.

Those with this disease describe feelings insects scuttling beneath their skin and have mysterious sores that ooze out blue and white fibers, some as thick as spaghetti strands. Attempts to remove the fibers are said to elicit shooting pains radiating from the site.

The lesions range from minor to disfiguring in appearance and the fibers appear either as single strands or as bundles. Patients also sometimes report the presence of fibers or black granular specks on their skin even in the absence of lesions.

According to a news report from KTVU-TV in Oakland, CA, Former Oakland A's pitcher Billy Koch has the disease, as does his wife and three children. Koch had to leave baseball at age 29 partly because of the uncontrollable muscle twitching that went on for months at a time and kept up him up all night.

The couple was at their wit's end after numerous doctors not only provided little in the way of relief, but actually were skeptical about their health problems. The Kochs may be the most recognizable of more than 3,000 families nationwide reporting these same unexplained symptoms. However, there are curious clusters of those suffering from the disease, in Florida along the Gulf Coast of Texas, and in California's San Francisco Bay Area.

To date, no clinical studies have looked into Morgellons and the first paper mentioning Morgellons was published in a recent issue of the ***American Journal of Clinical Dermatology***, co-authored by members of the Morgellons Research Foundation, a non-profit organization devoted to raising public awareness about the disease. The disease is named after a medical condition described in 1674 by the British author Thomas Browne. Known as "Morgellons," Browne said the disorder caused children to "critically break out with harsh hairs on their backs." However, the Morgellons Research Foundation says that it is doubtful that the 17th-century disease is related to modern-day Morgellons.

Analysis of the fibers found in the sores suggest that they are more than just lint from clothing, carpets, or bedding, nor are the black specks composed of pepper, as several dermatologists have proposed. Some suggest the fibers are made of cellulose, a molecule generally found in plants. And if placed in a petri dish, the fibers taken from a Margellons sore will continue to grow.

Surprisingly, most of the medical community seems to think that Morgellons is mass delusion and most people complaining of the symptoms are diagnosed with "delusional parasitosis," a psychological problem in which people imagine that they are infested with parasites. Yet patients a continent apart have reported the same symptoms long before hearing about the disease in the media or talking to other patients with similar symptoms.

THE MYSTERY DISEASE

According to a June, 2006 report on KHOU-TV in Houston, Texas, 59-year-old Cheryall Spiller suffers from what she believes is a mystery disease.

"Small white worms that come out of my ears, you can feel them itching in there. You can get a Q-tip and dig them out," she explained.

Spiller is not alone with her complaints. Other people also say that they have something strange under their skin.

The Final Nail In Your Coffin!

"The sores come up and these fuzzy, thread-like things come out," said Stephanie Bailey, Austin resident. "It's almost like spores or something like that."

Lesions and scars cover Stephanie Bailey's arms and legs. Travis Wilson is a victim as well.

"It feels just like bugs are crawling all over you. You can't sleep. It's freaky. So he'd go days without sleep," said Lisa Wilson, the patient's mother.

According to nurse practitioner Ginger Savely, all three may have an emerging sickness called Morgellons disease.

"It just looks you know like somebody picked at something and it got a little infected," Savely said.

Sufferers of Mogellons have taken their complaints to doctors. When magnified 60 times, the sores take on a completely different look.

"So you focus a little more you can see the black fibers the white fibers," Savely said.

Savely admitted the idea of creatures living inside our bodies seems more like science fiction than science.

"I don't think a person can believe it until they see it with their own eyes," she said. "The problem is people aren't looking hard enough, most practitioners are not looking because they are not taking them seriously."

Mainstream medical professionals don't believe Morgellons is real.

"I think if we look at what is truly evidence-based medicine, what has been proven based on scientific fact we know we don't have a means to substantiate her observations," said Dr. Adelaide Hebert, U.T. Health Science Center Houston.

Dr. Adelaide Hebert said Morgellons exists only in the patient's mind.

"Many of these patients do have delusion of parasitosis," Dr. Hebert said. "It is actually not uncommon to have patients come in and describe the sensation that something is crawling on their skin."

KHOU-TV searched for a Houston doctor who believes in or treats Morgellons, but none could be found. At Oklahoma State University research is currently underway on a volunteer basis. Ginger Savely has documented 100 cases and treats her patients with oral and topical antibiotics.

"They can't get anybody to help them in the medical profession. It's just a nightmare, a living nightmare. I can't imagine any worse disease," she said.

Lisa Wilson's son became so distraught about his condition he took his own life two weeks ago.

"He would tell me he'd rather have cancer because then he'd know what he was up against," Lisa Wilson said.

"They're worried about the bird flu coming, you've got something here right now that's spreadable and it's being hush-hushed," Spiller said.

"They told me I was doing it to myself and that I was nuts," Bailey explained. "I stopped going to doctors because I was afraid they were going to lock me up."

For most doctors, Morgellons is a textbook example of a type of mental illness where the victim believes that they are covered in parasites. This belief among doctors is so prevalent that few even bother to take the time to interview the sufferers of Morgellons, much less examine their skin lesions or look at the strange threads and fibers that ooze from their ulcers. However, Morgellons, or the Fiber Disease as some are calling it, is quickly spreading across the planet and the media is finally taking notice.

FORMER OAKLAND A'S PITCHER HAS MORGELLONS

As mentioned at the beginning of this chapter, former Oakland A's pitcher Billy Koch and his family has Morgellons. And though they can afford top medical care, doctors have no answers according to a news report by KTVU.

It started in Oakland four years ago. Koch saved 44 games and was the top reliever in the major leagues. His fastball wowed crowds. And then the strangeness began.

"He freaked out. He wanted to ignore it I wanted to too. But when it comes to your kids, you gotta stop ignoring it," said Koch's wife Brandi.

She describes their symptoms: "It was the scariest thing I had ever realized in my entire life. There were threads and black specks coming out and off of my skin."

Within two years, at age 29, Billy Koch was out of baseball, partly because of the uncontrollable muscle twitching that went on for months at a time and often kept up him up all night. The disease is characterized by slow healing skin lesions that often extrude small, dark filaments, especially after bathing.

"That's when it would really just ooze, literally ooze out of my skin," explained Brandi Koch.

The couple was at wit's end after numerous doctors not only provided little in the way of relief, but actually were skeptical about their health problems: "There's no reasonable explanation for it. I'm not seeing things. I'm watching it happen. We're pretty sane people" lamented Billy.

Infectious disease specialist Dr. Neelam Uppal sympathized with the Kochs' plight: "They've seen several doctors, and everybody's told them they're crazy. It's all in their head. They're delusional. That is the doctors that took the time to see them; most would not even bother to see their patients."

Dr. Uppal gave the Kochs and fifteen other patients a powerful anti-parasite medicine and antibiotics that helped temporarily. But the filaments come back.

Testing of the filaments brought no results, according to Dr. Uppal: "I've seen it; sent it to the lab. They can't identify it. They'll say 'They're nothing.'"

The reaction of medical professionals has made a difficult situation even harder for Brandi Koch: "It's not enough that you're suffering and hurting. It's 'You're an idiot!' and 'You're crazy!' on top of it. I'm really hurt and sad and scared."

The Kochs may be the most recognizable of more than 3,000 families nationwide reporting these same unexplained symptoms. There are curious clusters, in Florida, along the Gulf Coast and in the San Francisco Bay Area.

San Francisco physician Rafael Stricker took samples in the spring of 2006 from Bay Area sufferers. Patients report pustules and filaments that most doctors dismiss. Dermatologists claimed the filaments were all delusions, although none had studied them.

Oklahoma State University Professor Randy Wymore was the first scientist to conduct research on this disconcerting disease. He says it is the biggest mystery he's ever been involved in.

The UC Davis trained physiologist is leading a medical team at Oklahoma State University in Tulsa, researching the bizarre disease. With cooperation from the Centers for Disease Control and Prevention, Wymore's team is studying Bay Area patients and others from around the country. His first finding disputes the frequent diagnosis of delusions of parasites.

"Pathologists and dermatologists and lab reports said that these were textile fibers appearing in the skin of the sufferers: pieces of lint, threads from clothes or carpeting. Now that's just not true, to be perfectly blunt about it," says Prof. Wymore.

Wymore says his tests rule out not only textile fibers, but also worms, insects, animal material and even human skin and hair. He says the filaments are not an external contamination.

Instead, they are a substance that materializes somehow inside the body, apparent artifacts of something infectious. More results are expected soon. And Wymore says skin problems are not the worst symptoms.

He says a neurotoxin or microorganism may disturb muscle control and memory.

"The neurological effects are the much more severe, life altering and much more dangerous of the conditions," explains Prof. Wymore.

In June of 2006, Georgia began a statewide Morgellons registry. Prof. Wymore says he is about to begin a clinical trial and offers this to sufferers: "We know there's something going on here. You're not delusional."

Prof. Wymore has released an open letter to doctors treating patients with Morgellons symptoms. It asks physicians to take it seriously, saying these patients are likely suffering from a still untreatable emerging disease.

******

The Final Nail In Your Coffin!

May 15, 2006

Re: Morgellons Disease

From: Randy S. Wymore, Ph.D., Department of Pharmacology & Physiology, Rhonda Casey, D.O., Department of Pediatrics

Oklahoma State University Center for Health Sciences, Tulsa, Oklahoma

Dear Practitioner,

This letter concerns a patient population that manifests a particular set of symptoms we have encountered with increasing frequency, and that OSU-CHS is actively researching. The condition has been labeled as Morgellons Disease and it is unclear if this is a single disease or a multi-faceted syndrome.

Until recently, most of these patients have been grouped as a subset of the diagnosis of Delusions of Parasites (delusional parasitosis; DOP). After obtaining careful patient histories and thorough physical exam, we have determined that Morgellons patients have several important distinctions ruling out the diagnosis of DOP.

This population of patients frequently exhibits the following symptoms:

• Distinct and poorly healing skin lesions with unusually thick, membranous scarring upon eventual healing.

• Moderate to extreme pruritis at sites of lesions as well as un-erupted skin.

• Microscopic examination of these lesions will most often reveal the presence of unusual fibers, which may be black, blue or red. These fibers, which many healthcare providers initially thought to be textile contaminants, are often present in the deep tissue of biopsies obtained from unbroken skin of individuals with this condition. Careful examination of these fibers further reveals that they are frequently associated with hair follicles, and are definitely not textile in origin.

• Most of these patients suffer from a host of neurological symptoms which can vary in severity from mild to severe. These neurological symptoms include peripheral tingling, paresthesias and varying degrees of motor involvement which appear to progress.

• Intermittent cognitive and behavioral status changes are often observed and also seem to progress with the severity of disease. This is often referred to as "brain fog" by the patient as they experience a waxing and waning of this symptom.

• Laboratory findings in these patients are variable, but often reveal eosinophilia and elevated levels of Immunoglobin E.

• Other symptoms of varying severity and frequency have been described, and are included in the attached case definition.

Morgellons patients differ from classical, delusional parasitosis patients in several areas. They do not respond to antipsychotics, and new lesions continue to appear upon complete cessation of manual excoriation.

Due to the sensation of foreign material in their tissue, that has been described as sharp, stinging and/or splinter-like, the patient may have discovered the fibers prior to seeking medical care, and may bring them to your office for examination. Please do not assume that the patient's problem is purely psychological based on this propensity.

Many of these patients may appear skeptical of traditional medical care due to frequent dismissal of their symptoms in the past. The combination of suffering from a chronic disease with distressful symptoms and no known cause or cure can cause some patients to appear anxious or agitated.

We encourage you to take the time to carefully interview any patient who may fall into this category, perform any testing you may deem appropriate, and most importantly treat the patient with compassion and dignity.

Sincerely,

Randy S. Wymore, Ph.D.

Rhonda Casey, D.O.

Director of Research,

Associate Professor of Pediatrics

Morgellons Research Foundation

Assistant Professor of Pharmacology

Oklahoma State University - Center for Health Sciences

1111 West 17th Steet, Tulsa, Oklahoma 74107-1898

E-mail: morgellons@okstate.edu

Morgellons Information Line: (877) 599-7999

www.healthsciences.okstate.edu/morgellons/index.cfm

******

A TYPICAL CASE

Another typical case is Betty Armour, who is afraid to wear shorts and afraid of what people might think if they saw her condition. She is afraid of what they might say to her if she told them her truth.

"I have Morgellons disease," she would say.

From the knees down, Armour isn't herself, and she hasn't been for two and a half years. The fronts of her legs are noticeably discolored and bruised. It's a mixture of brown and purplish-looking scar tissue with pimply sores that itch and sting sometimes, says the 42-year-old Armour.

The wounds are so close together, they look like trails leading nowhere. "I think they have a wiry, suture quality to them," she said.

The Rancho Cucamonga, California woman has had similar, bizarre skin "lesions," for lack of a more descriptive or all-encompassing word, on her ankles, arms, breasts and hands. Painful sores on the tips of her fingers swelled up over Armour's nails and obstructed regular growth. Picking at them helped relieve tension, she says; today, they look fairly healthy.

She had similar swelling on her feet; her shoe size has gone from size 8 to 10.

At first, Armour thought she had come down with her second bout of lichen planus, a relatively common skin disease that afflicted her 15 years ago and is possibly linked to stress, experts say. Lichen planus usually fades, however, and although Armour's lesions have changed over time, they certainly aren't all gone.

Fruitless research ensued until a May 20, 2006 television broadcast on a local station opened Armour's eyes to Morgellons. Further, she found there to be more than 4,500 registered households listed on the Morgellons Research Foundation Web site.

The segment touched upon most of the symptoms Armour says she suffers, such as fatigue, joint pain and difficulty concentrating. This trio is so debilitating sometimes, a career beyond taking care of her teenagers – ages 15, 17, 19 – and miniature poodle seems like a pipe dream.

Before her health problems began, Armour, who grew up in La Puente, was an administrator at an area Longs Drugs distribution center for nearly a decade.

"I look forward to getting back to work, but I wouldn't hire me right now," Armour said.

According to research published in the American Journal of Clinical Dermatology, Morgellons disease is characterized by poorly healing skin lesions with thick, membranous scarring as well as fiberlike strands extruding from the lesions. Armour describes her fibers, which come off pretty easily, as cottonlike, fuzzy and many shades: beige, black, green and white. She's retained fiber samples in Ziploc bags and plastic containers, including "suturelike" fibers she's coughed up.

"It's getting very frustrating when people tell me I don't know what I'm talking about," she said. "I know it's real, I have the evidence."

Armour's children live with her, hug her and, fortunately, have not exhibited any of the six characteristic symptoms of Morgellons, as defined in the research foundation's case definition presented to the Centers for Disease Control and Prevention on Feb. 14, 2006:

1. Intensely itchy skin lesions, both appearing spontaneously and self-generated.

2. Crawling sensations conceptualized by the patient as bugs moving, stinging or biting, intermittently.

3. Fatigue.

4. Cognitive difficulties.

5. Behavioral effects, as many Morgellons patients have been diagnosed with attention-deficit (hyperactivity) disorder, bipolar disorder, obsessive-compulsive disorder or something similar.

6. Fibers.

Limited research has tried to link the skin ailment to Lyme disease as well as antibacterial therapy. Since Armour began seeking treatment two and a half years ago, physicians at her usual medical facility - PrimeCare of Inland Valley in Rancho Cucamonga - have neither alleviated her symptoms nor diagnosed her with anything more than dermatitis.

"I brought up Morgellons with one doctor," she said, "but he thought I was bonkers and wouldn't hear of it."

Without public outreach, Armour can't do much but wait. She longs to, but hasn't met or talked with anyone who suffers her symptoms. She wants to meet other with Morgellons and figure out what may have caused the disease, what the common denominators are.

Practically all sufferers of Morgellons are reluctant to talk about their illness because they know that some people would think they are crazy. And that is exactly what most doctors do think: As far as they know, Morgellons is not a recognized disease, at this point, at least.

"I've seen colors of some of these fibers. Some of them are bright blue," said Dr. Vincent De Leo, program director of the dermatology department at St. Luke's-Roosevelt Hospital Center in New York.

"There is nothing in the body that is bright blue. So it has to be something from the environment. And some of them are fibers, but they're fibers I believe from the environment, not from inside the skin."

De Leo and many others believe the lesions are self-inflicted, caused by scratching because the patients have a psychiatric disorder where they wrongly believe their bodies are infested with parasites.

"And then they begin to focus on those lesions and try to get them better, usually by picking out the fibers or the bugs or whatever it is," De Leo said.

Morgellons exhibits such bizarre symptoms that it is no wonder that physicians fail to recognize it as a real disease. Perhaps that is the plan by those who want the disease to spread unnoticed and unchecked until it is finally too late.

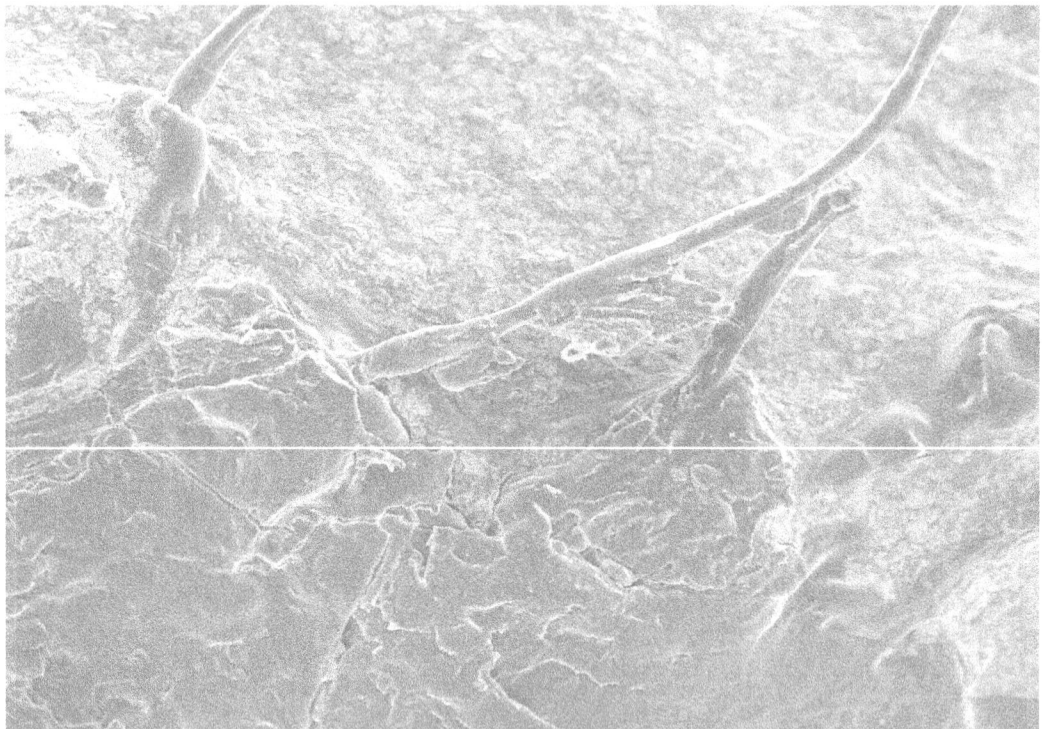

Bizarre thread-like fibers are one of the symptoms of Morgellons. Seen here under an electron microscope emerging from the skin.

CHAPTER TWO

The Biowarfare Conspiracy

THERE is a long and sordid history of the manmade manipulation of natural diseases for the use in war. It is natural to suspect any strange illness that seems to surface out of nowhere as the product of a mad experiment gone wrong and released on an unsuspecting population.

Take for example the latest manmade disease created by Mark Buller of the University of St Louis. His team deliberately produced an extremely lethal form of mousepox, a relative of the smallpox virus, one of the most deadly viruses on earth.

Financed by the National Institute of Allergy and Infectious Diseases, the research project was supposed to help find new protection against smallpox, which kills one in three victims. Unfortunately, it seems that there may have been other motives for the development of this virus.

Buller's new genetically altered mousepox virus kills all mice, even if they have been given antiviral drugs and a vaccine which would normally protect them. In addition, the cowpox virus, which also infects humans, has also been genetically manipulated under the pretense "that this work is necessary to explore what bioterrorists might do," says Buller.

According to **New Scientist**, Ian Ramshaw of the Australian National University said, "I have great concern about doing this in a pox virus that can cross species."

It has long been suspected that the HIV virus that causes AIDS was created for the use in biowarfare. This has long been the poster child for conspiracy theorists worldwide; however, respected doctors and scientists also suspect that there is more to HIV than a simple cross-species transference.

The first African woman to win the Nobel Peace Prize, Wangari Maatha of Kenya, has spoken out on the AIDS virus saying it was man-made and deliberateloy created as a weapon of biowarfare.

"In fact it (the HIV virus) is created by a scientist for biological warfare," she said. "Why has there been so much secrecy about AIDS? When you ask: where did the virus come from? it raises a lot of flags. That makes me suspicious," Maathai said.

The Kenya based **East Africa Standard** reported that in response to questions from Asian and European media, she said, "I want to dedicate the prize the African woman. I want to hold and embrace her. She has suffered so much and I feel this is an honor to her."

"Although I am a biologist, I have not done any research. I may not be able to say who developed the (HIV) virus but it was meant to wipe out the Black race," she continued.

When she first blamed the HIV/Aids on "some sadistic scientists, Professor Maathai kicked a storm, leaving some experts outraged and others supporting her," the Standard reported.

AIDS AS A WEAPON

William Campbell Douglass, MD, in his article **WHO Murdered Africa (The Man Made Origin of AIDS)** says that the World Health Organisation in published articles, called for scientists to work with deadly agents such as retro viruses and attempt to make a hybrid virus that would be deadly to humans.

In the bulletin of the World Health Organisation WHO), Volume 47, p.259, 1972, they said, "An attempt should be made to see if viruses can in fact exert selective effects on immune function. The possibility should be looked into that the immune response to the victims itself may be impaired if the infecting virus damages, more or less selectively, the cell responding to the virus."

What the WHO is saying in plain English is "Let's cook up a virus that selectively destroys the T-cell system of man, an acquired immune deficiency." In other words, AIDS.

Dr. Boyd E. Graves postulates that AIDS was the culmination of biowarfare research conducted by the U.S. Government (and later, by the Soviet government) throughout the 20th century. He believes AIDS was developed and proliferated for the primary purpose of wiping out blacks, homosexuals, and other social groups considered being "excess population."

Dr. Graves has also suggested that Gulf War syndrome may be related to AIDS which was spread by contaminating soldiers with vaccines, and that an effective cure for AIDS has already been developed and patented but is being withheld. The evidence Graves cites that AIDS was developed in U.S. was based on a 1971 Special Virus Cancer Flow Chart that he obtained through the Freedom of Information Act.

Graves claims to have contracted AIDS, but was cured by a single injection of Tetrasilver Tetroxide (Ag404) - not colloidal silver (see U.S. Patent #5,676,977 "Method of curing AIDS with tetrasilver tetroxide molecular crystal devices" held by Marantech. Graves, however, admits his diagnosis may have been a false positive. However, the claims made in the patent have not been investigated by any mainstream scientific body.

Dr. Alan Cantwell, author of *AIDS and the Doctors of Death: An Inquiry into the Origin of the AIDS Epidemic*, and, *Queer Blood: The Secret AIDS Genocide Plot*, believes that HIV is a genetically modified organism developed by U.S. Government scientists; that it was introduced into the population through Hepatitis B experiments performed on gay and bisexual men between 1978-1981 in Manhattan, Los Angeles, San Francisco, St. Louis, Denver, and Chicago. Cantwell claims these experiments were directed by Dr. Wolf Szmuness; and that there is an ongoing government and media cover-up regarding the origin of the AIDS epidemic.

Matilde Krim, a cancer virologist, AIDS expert, and the co-chairperson of the American Foundation for AIDS Research, has also suggested that Dr. Wolf Szmuness' hepatitis B vaccination experiments of the late 70's caused the

AIDS epidemic. Unlike Cantwell, however, she attributes this to accident rather than conspiracy.

Dr. Gary Glum claims in his book *Full Disclosure* that he received top secret information that AIDS was made in the laboratory at Cold Spring Harbor, New York. The virus was spread by putting the AIDS viruses into the smallpox eradication program by the World Health Organization, and that AIDS did not exist before 1978.

AIDS, he claims, was created for population control, especially of Blacks, Asians, and other colored people. The people who control the project were people known as the Olympians (another name for the Illuminati), who are also supporting eugenics. Organizations such as Red Cross are, according to Glum, complicit in the conspiracy by not testing blood properly. Glum also believes that AIDS can be transmitted through kissing, mosquito bites and casual contact.

Glum reports that Upjohn Pharmaceuticals tested a number of substances that can treat AIDS, but that the results have been suppressed. Much of Glum's evidence is based upon anecdotal claims, and critics have reported a complete absence of medical evidence to support his claims.

THE SICKENING HISTORY OF BIOWARFARE

Dr. Leonard G. Horowitz, author of *Emerging Viruses: AIDS & Ebola, Nature, Accident or Intentional?* and *Death in the Air: Globalism, Terrorism and Toxic Warfare*, has advanced the theory that the AIDS virus was engineered by such U.S. Government defense contractors as Litton Bionetics for the purposes of bio-warfare and "population control."

Dr. Horowitz believes that Jews, blacks, and Hispanics are prime targets in these attempts at "population control." He cites the historical preoccupation with eugenics on the part of the American medical establishment as evidence of a greater conspiracy to commit genocide.

It should be pointed out that the former Soviet Union, in a plot to destabilize the Western world, planted disinformation suggesting the CIA or other agencies created AIDS. According to KGB defector Vasili Mitrokhin, the KGB originated the claim through an East German physicist, Jakob Segal, in the mid 1980s. Because of this, any evidence that a new disease is a manmade conspiracy should always be treated with caution.

Biological warfare, also known as germ warfare, is the use of any organism (bacteria, virus or other disease-causing organism) or toxin found in nature, as a weapon of war. It is meant to incapacitate or kill an adversary. The creation and stockpiling of biological weapons is outlawed by the 1972 Biological Weapons Convention, signed by over 100 states, because a successful attack could conceivably result in thousands, possibly even millions, of deaths and could cause severe disruptions to societies and economies. Oddly enough, the convention prohibits only creation and storage, but not usage, of these weapons. However, the consensus among military analysts is that, except in the context of bioterrorism, biological warfare is militarily of little use.

The main problem is that a biological warfare attack would take days to implement, and therefore, unlike a nuclear or chemical attack, would not immediately stop an advancing army. As a strategic weapon, biological warfare is again militarily problematic, because unless it is used to poison enemy civilian towns, it is difficult to prevent the attack from spreading, either to allies or to the attacker, and a biological warfare attack invites immediate massive retaliation, usually in the same form.

The use of biological agents is not new, but before the 20th century, biological warfare took three main forms:

- Deliberate poisoning of food and water with infectious material.
- Use of microorganisms, toxins or animals, living or dead, in a weapon system.
- Use of biologically inoculated fabrics.

Biological warfare has been practiced repeatedly throughout history. During the 6th Century B.C., The Assyrians poisoned enemy wells with a fungus that would make the enemy delusional and unable to fight in battle. In 184 BC, Hannibal of Carthage had clay pots filled with poisonous snakes and instructed his soldiers to throw the pots onto the decks of Pergamene ships.

Historical accounts from medieval Europe detail the use of infected animal carcasses, by Mongols, Turks and other groups, to infect enemy water supplies. Prior to the bubonic plague epidemic known as the Black Death,

Mongol and Turkish armies were reported to have catapulted diseased corpses into besieged cities.

During the Middle Ages, victims of the bubonic plague were used for biological attacks, often by flinging their corpses and excrement over castle walls using catapults. The last known incident of using plague corpses for biological warfare occurred in 1710, when Russian forces attacked the Swedes by using catapults to fling plague-infected corpses over the city walls of Reval.

Much, or even most of the Native American population was decimated after contact with the Old World due to the introduction of many different fatal diseases. The British army at least once used smallpox as weapon, when they gave contaminated blankets to the Lenape. It is suspected but not confirmed that biological warfare was used against the Indians at other times as well.

Native peoples in Aptos gave to Spaniards gifts of freshly cut flowers wrapped in leaves of poison oak.

During the United States Civil War, General Sherman reported that Confederate forces shot farm animals in ponds upon which the Union depended for drinking water.

Use of such weapons was banned in international law by the Geneva Protocol of 1925. The 1972 Biological and Toxin Weapons Convention extended the ban to almost all production, storage and transport. It is, however, believed that since the signing of the convention the number of countries capable of producing such weapons has increased.

During the Sino-Japanese War (1937-1945) and World War II, Unit 731 of the Imperial Japanese Army conducted human experimentation on thousands, mostly Chinese. In military campaigns, the Japanese army used biological weapons on Chinese soldiers and civilians.

This employment was largely viewed as ineffective due to inefficient delivery systems. However, new information has surfaced within the last decade, which alleges a more active Japanese usage. For example, firsthand accounts testify the Japanese infected civilians through the distribution of plagued foodstuffs, such as dumplings, rice, bread and vegetables.

There are also reports of contaminated water supplies. Such estimates report over 580,000 victims, largely due to plague and cholera outbreaks. In addition, repeated seasonal outbreaks after the conclusion of the war bring the death toll much higher.

In response to suspected biological weapons development in Germany and Japan, the United States, United Kingdom, and Canada initiated a BW development program in 1941 that resulted in the weaponization of anthrax, brucellosis, and botulinum toxin. The center for U.S. military BW research was Fort Detrick, Maryland. Some biological and chemical weapons defense research was also conducted at Dugway Proving Grounds in Utah. Research carried out in the United Kingdom during World War II left a Scottish Island contaminated with anthrax for the next 48 years.

When biological and chemical weapons become too old, they sometimes need to be disposed of. Many NATO nations use the U.S. chemical weapons disposal facility on the tiny Johnston Atoll located in the middle of the Pacific.

Considerable research on the topic was performed by the United States, the Soviet Union, and probably other major nations throughout the Cold War era, though it is generally believed that such weapons were never used. This view was challenged by China and North Korea, who accused the United States of large-scale field testing of biological weapons against them during the Korean War (1950-1953).

Their accusation is substantiated by Stephen Endicott and Edward Hagerman in **The United States and Biological Warfare: secrets of the early Cold War and Korea** (Bloomington, Indiana University Press, 1998). In 1972, the U.S. signed the Biological and Toxic Weapons Convention, which banned "development, production, stockpiling, and use of microbes or their poisonous products except in amounts necessary for protective and peaceful research."

In 1986, the U.S. government spent $42 million on research for developing defenses against infectious diseases and toxins, ten times more money than was spent in 1981. The money went to 24 U.S. universities in hopes of developing strains on anthrax, Rift Valley fever, Japanese encephalitis, tularemia, shigella, botulin, and Q fever. When the Biology Department at MIT voted to refuse Pentagon funds for biotech research, the Reagan administration forced it to reverse its decision by threatening to cut off other funds.

There have been reports that the United States Army has been developing weapons-grade anthrax spores at Dugway Proving Ground, a chemical and biological defense testing facility in Utah, since at least as early as 1992. Under the BWC, nations are permitted to develop small amounts of BW agents for the purpose of defensive research. The United States maintains a stated national policy of never using biological weapons under any circumstances since November 1969 President Nixon.

BIOLOGICAL WEAPONS CHARACTERISTICS

Ideal characteristics of biological weapons are high infectivity, high potency, availability of vaccines, and delivery as an aerosol. Diseases most likely to be considered for use as biological weapons are contenders because of their lethality (if delivered efficiently), and robustness (making aerosol delivery feasible). The biological agents used in biological weapons can often be manufactured quickly and easily. The primary difficulty is not the production of the biological agent but delivery in an infective form to a vulnerable target.

For example, anthrax is considered an excellent agent. We use it here for discussion because it is historically important, and enough information is public that this discussion can't be used as a manual. First, it forms hardy spores, perfect for dispersal aerosols.

Second, pneumonic (lung) infections of anthrax usually do not cause secondary infections in other people. Thus, the effect of the agent is usually confined to the target. A pneumonic anthrax infection starts with ordinary "cold" symptoms and quickly becomes lethal, with a fatality rate that is 80% or higher. Finally, friendly personnel can be protected with suitable antibiotics or vaccines.

A mass attack using anthrax would require the creation of aerosol particles of 1.5 to 5 micrometres. Too large and the aerosol would be filtered out by the respiratory system. Too small and the aerosol would be inhaled and exhaled. Also, at this size, nonconductive powders tend to clump and cling because of electrostatic charges. This hinders dispersion. So, the material must be treated with silica to insulate and discharge the charges. The aerosol must be delivered so that rain and sun does not rot it, and yet the human lung can be infected. There are other technological difficulties as well.

Diseases considered for weaponization, or known to be weaponized include anthrax, Ebola, Bubonic Plague, Cholera, Tularemia, Brucellosis, Q fever, Machupo, VEE, and Smallpox. Naturally-occurring toxins that can be used as weapons include Ricin, SEB, Botulism Toxin, and many Mycotoxins.

It is important to note that all of the classical and modern biological weapons organisms are animal diseases, the only exception being smallpox. Thus, in any use of biological weapons, it is highly likely that animals will become ill either simultaneously with, or perhaps earlier than humans.

In the largest biological weapons "accident" known, the anthrax outbreak in Sverdlovsk (now Yekaterinburg) in the Soviet Union in 1971, sheep became ill with anthrax as far as 200 kilometers from the release point of the organism from a military facility in the southeastern portion of the city (known as Compound 15 and still off limits to visitors today). As we all now know, anthrax is very effective as a biological terror weapon.

MORGELLONS AND LYME DISEASE

Often those unfortunate enough to suffer with the debilitating symptoms of Morgellons are also found to have contracted Lyme disease sometime in the past. Doctors are still trying to determine if there is a biological connection with the two, or if Morgellons is simply taking opportunity of an already compromised immune system.

It is interesting that there is a connection between Lyme disease and Morgellons. This considering the attention Lymes has garnered with certain health professionals who feel that Lymes is not an ordinary illness.

Dr. Donald MacArthur, who was in charge of the development and testing of biological weapons for the Pentagon, spoke at a hearing before a Subcommittee of the Committee on Appropriations in 1969. MacArthur puts it like this.

> "Incapacitating agents are a more recent development and are largely in the research and development phase (in 1969). In fact, the prime emphasis in agent research and development is on developing better incapacitating agents. We are synthesizing new compounds and testing them in animals. I should mention that there is a rule of thumb we use. Before an agent can be classified as an incapacitant, we feel that the mortality should be very low. Therefore, the ratio of the lethal dose to the incapacitating dose has to be very high. Now this is a very technical job. We have some of the top scientists in the

country working for years on how to get more effective incapacitating agents. It is not easy. An incapacitating agent imposes a greater logistic burden on the enemy when he has to look after the disabled people."

Dr. Joseph Burrascano, who has done extensive research on Lyme disease, presented testimony in 1993 to the Senate Hearing Committee on Lyme disease. Dr. Burrascano stated in his testimony that he feared repercussions for speaking out at the Hearing. Obviously his fears were justified as he was later investigated by the Office of Professional Medical Conduct in New York. Dr. Burrascano was finally vindicated and did not lose his license, but it raises questions on why doctors who treat and speak out about Lymes, are finding themselves in the crosshairs of government persecution.

✶✶✶✶✶✶

The Lyme Disease Conspiracy

By Joseph J. Burrascano, Jr., M.D.

Reprinted from Senate Committee Hearing on

Lyme Disease - August 5, 1993

There is a core group of university-based Lyme disease researchers and physicians whose opinions carry a great deal of weight. Unfortunately many of them act unscientifically and unethically. They adhere to outdated, self-serving views and attempt to personally discredit those whose opinions differ from their own. They exert strong ethically questionable influence on medical journals, which enables them to publish and promote articles that are badly flawed. They work with government agencies to bias the agenda of consensus meetings, and have worked to exclude from these meetings and scientific seminars those with alternate opinions. They behave this way for reasons of personal or professional gain, and are involved in obvious conflicts of interest.

This group promotes the idea that Lyme is a simple, rare illness that is easy to avoid, difficult to acquire, simple to diagnose, and easily treated and cured with 30 days or less of antibiotics.

The truth is that Lyme is the fastest growing infectious illness in this country after AIDS, with a cost to society measured in the billions of dollars. It can be acquired by anyone who goes outdoors, very often goes undiagnosed for months, years, or forever in some patients, and can render a patient chronically ill and even totally disabled despite what this core group refers to as "adequate" therapy. There have been deaths from Lyme disease.

They feel that when the patient fails to respond to their treatment regimens it is because the patient developed what they named "the post Lyme syndrome". They claim that this is not an infectious problem, but a rheumatologic or arthritic malady due to activation of the immune system.

The fact is this cannot be related to any consistent abnormality other than persistent infection. As further proof, vaccinated animals whose immune system has been activated by Lyme have never developed this syndrome. On the other hand, there is proof that persistent infection can exist in these patients because the one month treatment did not eradicate the infection.

Indeed, many chronically ill patients, whom these physicians dismissed, have gone on to respond positively and even recover, when additional antibiotics are given.

It is interesting that these individuals who promote this so called "post-Lyme syndrome" as a form of arthritis, depend on funding from arthritis groups and agencies to earn their livelihood. Some of them are known to have received large consulting fees from insurance companies to advise them to curtail coverage for any antibiotic therapy beyond this arbitrary 30 day cutoff, even if the patient will suffer. This is despite the fact that additional therapy may be beneficial, and despite the fact that such practices never occur in treating other diseases.

Following the lead of this group of physicians, a few state health departments have even begun to investigate, in a very threatening way, physicians who have more liberal views on Lyme disease diagnosis and treatment than they do. Indeed, I must confess that I feel that I am taking a large personal risk here today by publicly stating these views, for fear that I may suffer some negative repercussions, despite the fact that many hundreds of physicians and many thousands of patients all over the world agree with what I am saying here. Because of this bias by this inner circle, Lyme disease is both under diagnosed and undertreated, to the great detriment to many of our citizens. Let me address these points in more detail.

UNDER DIAGNOSIS

1. Under reporting: The current reporting criteria for Lyme are inadequate and miss an estimated 30 to 50% of patients. Some states curtailed their active surveillance programs and saw an artificial drop in reported cases of nearly 40%, leading the uninformed to believe incorrectly that the number of new cases of Lyme is on the decline. The reporting procedure is often so cumbersome that many physicians never bother to report cases. Some physicians have found themselves unexpectedly the target of state health department investigators. Finally, to many physicians and government agents rely on the notoriously unreliable serologic blood test to confirm the diagnosis.

2. Poor Lyme disease diagnostic testing: It is very well-known that the serologic blood test for Lyme is insensitive, inaccurate, not standardized, and misses up to 40 percent of cases, yet many physicians, including many of those referred to above, and the senior staff at CDC and NIH, insist that if the blood test is negative, then the patient could not possibly have Lyme. This view is not supported by the facts. Lyme is diagnosed clinically, and can exist even when the blood test is negative.

The Rocky Mountain Lab of the NIH, which is the country's best government laboratory for Lyme research, had developed an excellent diagnostic test for this illness nearly 4 years ago, yet further work on it has been stalled due to lack of funding. Incredibly, if not for private donations of just $5,000 from the non-profit National Lyme Disease Foundation headquartered in

Connecticut, then this research would have had to be abandoned. An additional $30,000 was donated by this organization to allow them to continue other valuable projects relating to vaccine development and disease pathogenesis. Yet, many physicians believe that thousands of dollars of grant moneys awarded by the government to other, outside researchers is poorly directed, supporting work of low relevance and low priority to those sick with Lyme. In spite of this, their funding continues, and the Rocky Mountain Lab is still underfunded.

3. The university and Government based Lyme establishment deny the existence of atypical presentations of Lyme and patients in this category are not being diagnosed or treated, and have no one to see and no place to go for proper care.

RESULTS: Some Lyme patients have had to see, as many as 42 different physicians often over several years, and at tremendous cost, before being properly diagnosed. Unfortunately, the disease was left to progress during that time, and patients were left forever ill, for by that time, their illness was not able to be cured. Even more disturbing, these hard line physicians have tried to dismiss these patients as having "Lyme Hysteria" and tried to claim they all were suffering from psychiatric problems!

UNDERTREATMENT

1. Because the diagnosis is not being made, for reasons partly outlined above.

2. University based and government endorsed treatment protocols are empiric, insufficient, refer to studies involving inadequate animal models, and are ignorant of basic pharmacology. They are not based on honest systematic studies or on the results of newer information.

3. After short courses of treatments with antibiotics, patients with advanced disease rarely return to normal, yet many can be proven to still be severely infected and can often respond to further, proper, antibiotic therapy. Unfortunately, many Lyme patients are being routinely denied such therapy for political

reasons and/or because insurance companies refuse to pay for longer treatment, upon the arbitrary and uninformed advice of these physicians, who are on the insurance company's payroll.

4. Long term studies on patients who were untreated or undertreated demonstrated the occurrence of severe illness more than a decade later, reminiscent of the findings of the notorious Tuskeege Study, in which intentionally untreated syphilis patients were allowed to suffer permanent and in some cases fatal sequelae.

5. The Lyme bacterium spreads to areas of the body that render this organism resistant to being killed by the immune system and by antibiotics, such as in the eye, deep within tendons, and within cells. The Lyme bacterium also has a very complex life cycle that renders it resistant to simple treatment strategies. Therefore, to be effective, antibiotics must be given in generous doses over several months, until signs of active infection have cleared. Because relapses have appeared long after seemingly adequate therapy, long term followup, measured in years or decades, is required before any treatment regimen is deemed adequate or curative.

6. When administered by skilled clinicians, the safety of long term antibiotic therapy has been firmly established.

The very existence of hundreds of Lyme support groups in this country, and the tens of thousands of dissatisfied, mistreated and ill patients whom these groups represent, underscores the many problems that exist out in the real world of Lyme disease. I ask and plead with you to hear their voices, listen to their stories, and work in an honest and unbiased way to help and protect the many Americans whose health is at risk from what now has become a political disease. Thank you.

******

As pointed out by the Morgellons Research Foundation, many patients with Morgellons disease have positive Western Blots for Borrelia burgdorferi, the causative agent of Lyme disease. It appears that there may be a connection between the two infectious diseases, with one agent possibly predisposing the individual to the second agent. Whether all patients with Morgellons disease also have Lyme borreliosis remains to be seen. There is some recent information that the fibrous, and other, material associated with skin lesions may be caused by an unknown viral agent or agents.

Ginger Savely, a family nurse practitioner working in a family practice clinic in Austin, Texas, has been seeing patients with Morgellons. These patients have come to her from all over the state of Texas, desperate for answers and willing to go anywhere to be treated with dignity and taken seriously. Savely continues to be impressed with the consistency of their stories. All but one of these patients have tested positive for Lyme borreliosis by Western Blot through IGeneX Laboratories in Palo Alto, California. When she treats these patients with antibiotics for their Lyme disease, she is also seeing remission in Morgellons symptoms in most of her patients.

The true prevalence of Lyme disease is much higher than is being reported by health officials. It is difficult to know how many cases are unreported but estimations suggest that the prevalence is actually 10-15 times higher than what is actually being reported.

Why are health official's under-reporting cases of Lyme disease? Again, the answer is because physicians don't recognize and report most cases. These misdiagnosed cases go unreported even though Lyme disease is a mandatory reportable disease (in the state of Iowa).

A futile cycle exists causing numerous cases of Lyme disease to be misdiagnosed and unreported. That is, since most cases of Lyme disease go undiagnosed, health officials under-report Lyme disease; thus, physicians that read their official reports believe that the prevalence of Lyme is rare and place it low on their list of possibilities when faced with clinical cases that could be caused by Borrelia.

The plague of ignorance surrounding Lyme disease makes it very controversial within the medical community. Most MDs are ignorant about the complex nature of Lyme disease and are frequently irritated when confronted about it.

There are only a few MDs in the country that are knowledgeable about Lyme disease; they are often called Lyme literate MDs (LLMDs) by the Lyme aware public and by their Lyme patients. Most LLMDs know about Lyme disease because they have studied it independently. The MD's formal training in medical school and from the established medical community regarding Lyme disease is meager.

LLMDs have been and continue to be harassed by the medical community, by health officials, by their peers and colleagues, by state medical boards, and by insurance companies for diagnosing and treating Lyme patients beyond the standards set by the establishment. Unfortunately, some of these LLMDs have discontinued treating Lyme patients due to the harassment.

A few LLMDs have actually had their medical license revoked because they have treated Lyme patients beyond standards set by the medical community. For example, treating patients with antibiotics for longer than the standard 4-6 week period of time can lead to harassment. A good example of this harassment is the case of Lida Mattman PhD, a microbiologist and author of Stealth Pathogens, was forced to close her Michigan lab in January, 2003. Dr. Mattman, who has studied spirochetes for fifty years, was told by the Michigan state attorney's office to stop helping physicians diagnose Lyme disease in patients, or risk jail time and/or a $5,000 a day fine.

Dr. Mattman has a protocol for culturing the blood of patients, even those who are seronegative for Lyme disease, and is able to find the spirochetes thriving in the blood after a few days incubation. She has helped many patients receive proper antibiotic treatment this way.

She says it has gotten increasingly difficult over the years, to find human negative controls in the U.S. to supply blood free of Borrelia. Dr. Mattman has also recently had the state police arrive at her lab with handcuffs, searching for evidence that she was still doing this work. Fortunately, they did not find the evidence that they were looking for.

Lyme disease affects the nervous system directly and indirectly through the production of neurotoxins. Many patients have had fatigue and poor sleep for years before presenting, and because of strange opportunistic skin infections, it is very easy to mistakenly diagnose them with delusions of parasites. Most labs have inadequate testing for Lyme. Further, there is no known adequate testing for the Piroplasmosis variants, and at least 13 are known to exist.

Those who are brave enough to report their symptoms of Morgellons, find startling similarities with the symptoms of Lyme disease. Symptoms can and may include (but not limited to) involuntary muscle twitches, chronic fatigue, inability to handle stress, low hormone levels, fibromyalgia, (pain and aching of nerve and muscles) muscle spasms, muscle and joint swelling, confusion, mental overload, difficulty concentrating, paralysis sensation, nausea.

Of particular concern with Morgellons is the possibility that it is contagious, unlike Lyme disease. There are cases in the country of multiple family members coming down with the same symptoms. In fact, there is a strong likelihood that if one family member has Morgellons, others will soon follow.

The states of California, Texas and Florida appear to have the highest number of reports of this disease, with primary clusters noted in Los Angeles, San Francisco, Houston, Dallas, and Austin, Texas. All fifty states and fifteen nations, including Canada, the UK, Australia and the Netherlands report cases of Morgellons. The total number of registrations to the Morgellons Research Foundation website is presently 1200, which is believed by the foundation to be a fraction of the actual number of cases.

The two main occupational groups reporting symptoms of Morgellons are nurses and teachers. Nurses outnumber teachers 3:1, but both occupational groups represent a significant percentage of patients with this disease. It is unclear what the risk factors for these two occupational groups might be, but the possibility of casual transmission of infectious agents has been entertained.

There is some evidence to suggest that skin lesions and fibers may not be readily apparent on all individuals with this disease, as family members of patients often report similar systemic disease symptoms, without skin symptoms. Whether the disease is transmissible by human contact remains unclear. Although most sufferers are fearful of infecting family members, families where all are affected are ones where simultaneous mutual exposure is suspected.

Patients have also reported symptoms of this disease in their pets. The majority of reports involve dogs, but cats appear to be increasingly affected. There have also been recent reports of horses with skin lesions fitting the description of Morgellons lesions. Several horse owners have observed fibers associated with skin lesions on their animals, by using lighted 30x handheld microscopes.

Dr. William Harvey is the current chairman of the NASA Education Advisory Committee. He has documented more than 565 of these (Borreliosis) cases in Texas and says 94% of (those with Morgellons' skin lesions) have tested positive for the bacteria associated with Lyme disease, or Borreliosis. "I think we are a looking at a major problem that has been unrecognized in humanity right now."

There has even been the suggestion that Morgellons is a weaponized version of Lyme disease. But where could such a disease be developed?

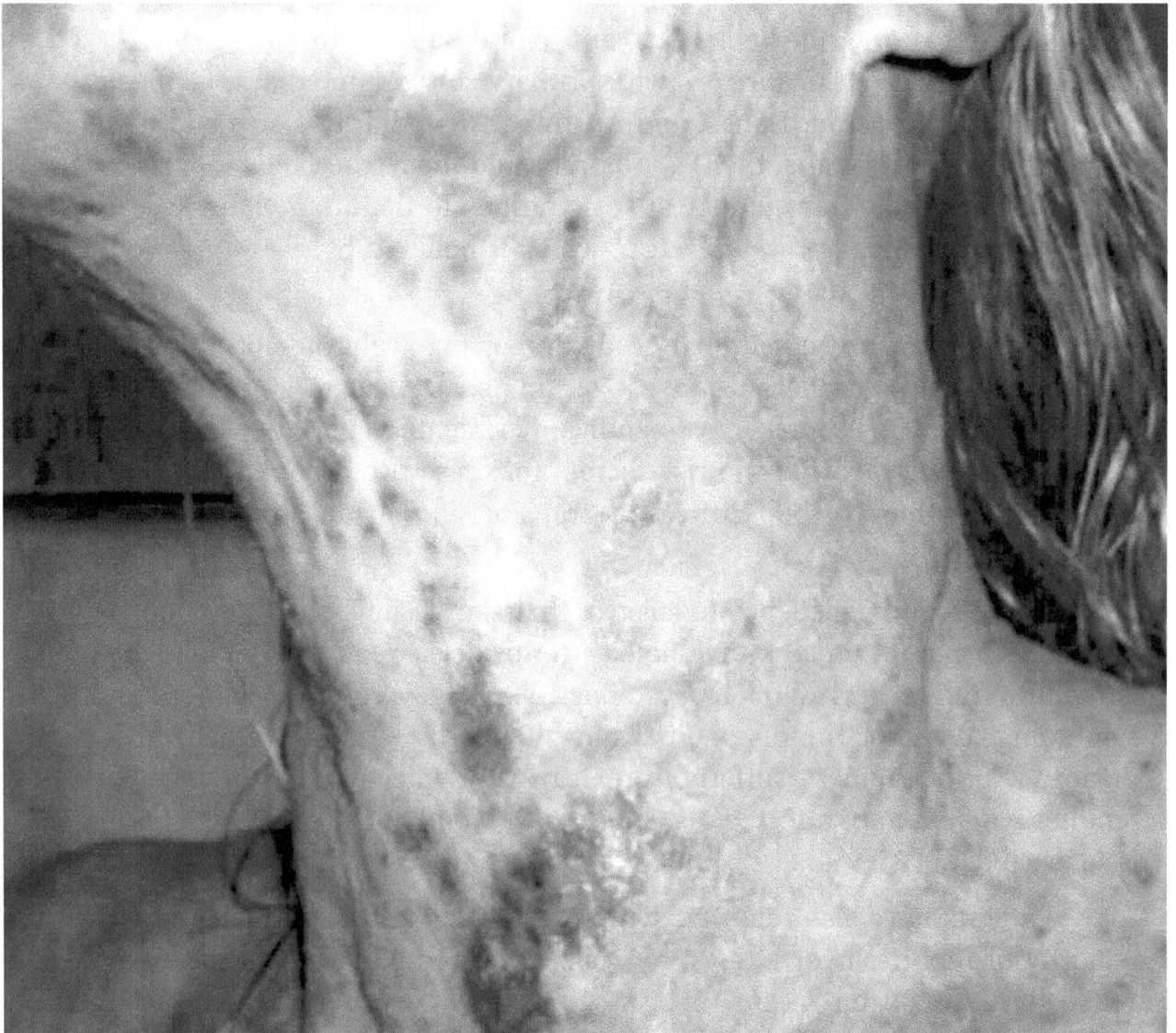

Those inflicted with Morgellons will suffer from persistent itchy sores and rashes all over the skin and often develop fiber like protrusions within their sores and the surrounding skin.

CHAPTER THREE

Was Morgellons Developed in A Lab?

THERE have been allegations over the years that Lyme disease was a natural disease made worse by genetic manipulation. The focus of these accusations is Plum Island, Just off Orient Point, Long Island, and six miles from the Connecticut coast.

Plum Island is the site of a United States Agriculture Department Animal Disease Research Center. The USDA acquired the island from the War Department at the end of World War II with a charter from Congress to study and eradicate animal diseases such as Foot and Mouth Disease.

In 1954, research was influenced by the Cold War and scientists began studying ways to inflict damage on Soviet livestock. The Cuban government alleges that in the 1960s and 70s, bioweapons developed at Plum were deployed against Cuban agriculture, targeting pork, tobacco and sugar cane.

Today, Plum Island is home to a Bio-Safety Level 4 (possibly a secret Bio-Safety 5) research facility. The only comparable government facilities in the country are the United States Army laboratory at Fort Detrick, MD, and the Centers for Disease Control and Prevention in Atlanta.

Plum Island is specifically engaged in the study of zoonotic diseases. Zoonotic diseases are diseases that can be transmitted from animals to humans, like West Nile, Lyme disease and Ebola. In surrounding communities, distrust of Plum Island runs deep. Lyme disease takes its name from a Connecticut town across from the island; many wonder whether birds or swimming animals could have brought the disease from Plum Island. Some suspect that it may have been deliberately released. Plum Island officials, of course, dismiss such hypotheses as fantasy.

Citizen concerns do, however, have validation. Even though it is located on an island, Plum Island's lab is not quarantined. Scientists and other laboratory workers commute to Connecticut and Long Island. In August 1994, a worker at Yale's Arbovirus Laboratory became infected with Sabia Virus but went home and then to Boston before realizing his symptoms was serious.

The risk of accidental exposure would be greater on Plum Island, where instead of cultures in flasks (as at Yale), there are animal populations infected with zoonotic diseases. Such diseases have incubation times of days; a worker could easily go home or travel without realizing that they had been infected.

The government claims that there has only been one outbreak on the island, Foot and Mouth in 1978, which they contained by killing all the livestock. They further maintain that there has never been a leak to the mainland. Apparently the first appearance of Lyme disease, 13-miles northeast of the facility, falls under the category of coincidence, as does the mysterious and still unexplained appearance of West Nile virus in Long Island and New York City.

Until 1991, all of the employees at Plum Island were federal. During 1991 and '92, the workforce divided, with many of the jobs being turned over to the private sector, which naturally led to a simmering resentment in the ranks.

On August 13, 2002, the resentment came to a full boil and a strike was called; 76 members of the International Union of Operating Engineers walked out at midnight after negotiations on wages and benefits broke down. The union members, employed by a government subcontractor, LB&B Associates, headquartered in Columbia, MD, were responsible for essential support services such as decontamination, waste-water treatment, keeping the generators in working order and other maintenance and safety-oriented occupations. For the duration of the strike, temps were brought in to replace them, the sentinels and technicians of the island's infrastructure.

By the end of that month, the FBI had been called to the island to investigate allegations of sabotage. It seems that the water pressure on the island fell precipitously, disabling decontamination facilities and the necropsy rooms used to examine dead animals.

The union blamed the problem on the inexperienced temporary replacement workers, suggesting that they had not been adequately screened and lacked the training to properly maintain the essential daily activity of the island, let alone handle an emergency. Jacob Bunch, a spokesman for LB&B, refused to comment on the FBI investigation and responded to a *New York Times* reporter's query about the replacement workers by stating that "In terms of training, I will tell you that people are well trained or they wouldn't be there. I am not going to get into how they are trained." He flatly refused to discuss the issue of security clearances.

Press requests to visit the island were denied by both the FBI and the USDA, but one union official claimed to have received a frantic call from one of the replacement workers. As he put it, "They were sleeping on cots, working 12-hour shifts and not being able to make calls off the island. He described their condition as being held captive." The chief operating officer of LB&B, Ed Brandon, scoffed at the report, saying that the worker in question had already left the island and that everything was under control and running smoothly.

As a result of the FBI investigation, one of the strikers, Mark J. DePonte, pleaded guilty to tampering with government property. Coincidentally, in October a 600-gallon container of liquid nitrogen somehow managed to tumble off the rear of one of the island's ferries. Shortly thereafter, it was revealed that at least one of the replacement workers had an arrest record.

SECRET WORK WITH MYCOPLASMA

There are 200 species of Mycoplasma. Most do no harm; only four or five are pathogenic. Mycoplasma fermentans (incognitus strain) probably comes from the nucleus of the Brucella bacterium. This disease agent is not a bacterium and not a virus; it is a mutated form of the Brucella bacterium, combined with a visna virus, from which the mycoplasma is extracted.

The pathogenic Mycoplasma used to be innocuous, but biological warfare research conducted between 1942 and the present time has resulted in the creation of more deadly and infectious forms of Mycoplasma. Researchers extracted this mycoplasma from the Brucella bacterium and actually reduced the disease to a crystalline form. It was then probably weaponised and tested it on an unsuspecting public in the United States.

Dr. LeeAnn Thomas, the previous Director of Plum Island, told author Marjorie Tietjen that Iraqi researcher, Dr. Jawad Al Aubaidi, (who has since been murdered) did his graduate training at Plum Island, specifically involving different strains of mycoplasma. He went back to Iraq and headed up the mycoplasma research program at the University of Bagdad.

Tiejen had been sent information from a reliable source that stated that 60% of chronic lyme patients are co-infected with several strains of mycoplasma, the most common one being "mycoplasma fermentens" which is patented by the U.S. Army and army pathologist Dr. Shyh-Ching Lo (Pathogenic mycoplasma-U.S. Patent 5,242,820 issued Sept. 7, 1993).

Tiejen writes in her article: ***Living Next Door To Plum Island*** that it is evident that any microbe that has been "modified" is considered "off limits" for treatment and any physician that takes these chronic infections seriously, is targeted for harassment. This same pathogen is found in Gulf War Illness, Fibromyalgia, Chronic Fatigue patients, and maybe Morgellons.

Tietjen asked Dr. Thomas if Plum Island ever worked with mycoplasmas in general. She denied this at the beginning but gradually admitted researching seven different strains. Tuethen asked if Plum Island researchers ever worked with mycoplasma fermentens. Dr. Thomas was immediately familiar with that particular genetically engineered strain although she did deny that Plum Island researchers ever worked with it.

According to accurate and verified accounts, Saddam Hussein purchased mycoplasma as well as other biologicals, which included West Nile Virus, from the U.S. right up to two weeks before Desert Storm.

West Nile virus infection in humans first broke out in New York City in August, 1999. The first sign of the disease occurred in early July when half the crows in the New York City area died, as well as some exotic bird species housed at the Bronx zoo.

A few weeks after the bird deaths, the first human cases of encephalitis appeared in local hospitals in the northern Queens section of the city. By September, nine of 25 infected horses with WN virus died in Long Island. It was later discovered that mosquito's acts as a carrier for the virus, thus it spreads from birds to mosquitoes. The virus then is spread to humans and other animals by mosquito bites.

Although the virus is contagious between birds, the disease is not contagious between humans. It is estimated that only 20% of infected people will develop a mild flu-like form of the illness; but one in 150 people will develop a severe form of the disease with mental confusion, headache, swollen glands, high fever, severe muscle weakness, and the tell-tale symptoms of encephalitis (inflammation of the brain). Mild cases last a few days; severe cases can last several weeks.

In 1999, the disease was completely confined to the New York City area, with 62 cases and 7 deaths. As many as 10,000 wild birds died. In the year 2000, there were 21 cases and two deaths; in 2001 there were 56 cases with 7 deaths. By October 8, 2002 the CDC had reported a cumulative total of 2768 cases of WN virus with 146 deaths; and it is estimated that as many as 200,000 people are infected nationally.

Until 2002 the virus was confined to states in the eastern half of the country. By the summer of 2002, all but 6 of the lower 48 states reported West Nile virus in birds, mosquitoes, animals or humans. It has caused nearly 17,000 cases of illness in people, more than 650 of them fatal.

Secret CIA documents point the finger at Iraq as being responsible for the West Nile virus outbreak in the United States. Health officials believe the West Nile virus may have been genetically altered into an illness far deadlier to human beings. Interestingly, the U.S. strain appears almost identical to only one other strain in the world – the one found in Israel.

In most parts of the world where it has surfaced, the virus typically causes illness akin to the flu, bringing fever, headache, muscle aches and fatigue – unpleasant, but rarely fatal. The virus has not even proven fatal to all birds in other parts of the world. But the U.S. strain appears nearly 100 percent fatal to birds. They usually die within five days.

Once again, this has caused some health officials and scientists, as well as intelligence sources, to wonder if West Nile Virus is not a weaponized virus – one perhaps deliberately engineered and delivered to the two biggest targets of Islamic terrorism. Israel was the first place in the world where West Nile virus was associated with killing birds. Until that outbreak in 1997, the virus was known to sicken birds, but not fatally. Israel also was the site of an outbreak of West Nile virus in humans that caused 450 cases of neurological disease in 2000.

While it is well-known that West Nile virus is of Middle East origin, what is less well-known is the New Yorker report dating back to 2000 in which Saddam Hussein was quoted by a defector referring to "his final weapon, developed in laboratories outside Iraq...free of U.N. inspection, the laboratories will develop strain SV 141 of the West Nile virus." There is also a report that the Centers for Disease Control actually sent West Nile virus samples to Iraq in 1985.

One entomology expert who maintains an open mind on the West Nile outbreak, Dr. Jonathan F. Day of the University of Florida, said: "The sporadic appearance of West Nile virus is disturbing. It really appears that the virus has been seeded throughout the eastern half of the United States. I guess the question is, by whom?"

It is not too far outside of the spectrum to suggest that Morgellons could be a manmade disease related to Lyme and West Nile. One woman, identified by the name "L," sent the author an e-mail stating that her husband, in 1993/1994, worked as a mechanical technician for a chemical plant that started an experimental program for their wastewater treatment plant adding plant organisms into their wastewater treatment facility.

"He assisted with the installation of the startup equipment and overlooked the ongoing maintenance of this equipment. There were times he would be working on this equipment in nothing more than rubber boots and a dust mask. This plant organism was not supposed to infect humans."

"L" and her husband have both come down with symptoms of Morgellons. From the research so far, scientists who are examining the lesions and the fibers extracted from them are finding that the fibers might be made of cellulose, a molecule generally found in plants.

Another source reported that Morgellons had been researched by the Chinese since 1994. Their findings were nematodes that had been genetically modified in the use at waste water treatment plants were the cause of the disease.

Nematodes are a good candidate for Mogellons, whether natural or genetically modified. They can be hard to spot, are sometimes infectious, have several species known to infest humans, and have produced other baffling cases.

One of the strangest cases is the multi-limbed frogs in Minnesota. Turns out, they were infested with nematodes while they were tadpoles; every spot where a nematode had lived for some reason developed into a leg when the frog metamorphosed into an adult. The reason they had suddenly become a problem was because of dramatic changes in the local ecosystem, mainly brought about by man, which led to a nematode population explosion.

CUSTOM-BUILT PATHOGENS RAISE BIOTERROR FEARS

The Washington Post reported on July 31, 2006 that terrorists could someday use a shortcut to get their hands on the lethal viruses that cause Ebola and smallpox. Eckard Wimmer knows this because he discovered it himself. In 2002, the German-born molecular geneticist startled the scientific world by creating the first live, fully artificial virus in the lab. It was a variation of the bug that causes polio, yet different from any virus known to nature. And Wimmer built it from scratch.

The virus was made from nonliving parts, using equipment and chemicals on hand in Wimmer's small laboratory at the State University of New York on Long Island. The most crucial part, the genetic code, was picked up for free on the Internet. Hundreds of tiny bits of viral DNA were purchased online, with final assembly in the lab.

Wimmer intended to sound a warning, to show that science had crossed a threshold into an era in which genetically altered and made-from-scratch germ weapons were feasible. But in the four years since, other scientists have made advances faster than Wimmer imagined possible. Government officials, and scientists such as Wimmer, are only beginning to grasp the implications.

The new technology opens the door to new tools for defeating disease and saving lives. But today, in hundreds of labs worldwide, it is also possible to transform common intestinal microbes into killers. Or to make deadly strains even more lethal...or to resurrect bygone killers, such the 1918 influenza...or to manipulate a person's hormones by switching genes on or off...or to craft cheap, efficient delivery systems that can infect large numbers of people.

The Final Nail In Your Coffin!

The U.S. Centers for Disease Control and Prevention has declined so far to police the booming gene-synthesis industry, which churns out made-to-order DNA to sell to scientists. Oversight of controversial experiments remains voluntary and sporadic in many universities and private labs in the United States, and occurs even more rarely overseas.

Wimmer's artificial virus looks and behaves like its natural cousin –but with a far reduced ability to maim or kill – and could be used to make a safer polio vaccine. However, it was Wimmer's techniques, not his aims that sparked controversy when news of his achievement reached the scientific journals.

As the creator of the world's first "de novo" virus – a human virus, at that–Wimmer came under attack from other scientists who said his experiment was a dangerous stunt. He was accused of giving ideas to terrorists, or, even worse, of inviting a backlash that could result in new laws restricting scientific freedom.

Wimmer counters that he didn't invent the technology that made his experiment possible. He only drew attention to it.

New techniques developed by other scientists allow the creation of synthetic viruses in mere days, not weeks or months. Hardware unveiled last year by a Harvard genetics professor can churn out synthetic genes by the thousands, for a few pennies each.

In less than five years, synthetic biology has gone from a kind of scientific parlor trick, useful for such things as creating glow-in-the-dark fish, to a cutting-edge bioscience with enormous commercial potential. Now the technology can be even done at the lab bench in high school.

Along with synthetic biologists, a separate but equally ardent group is pursuing DNA shuffling, a kind of directed evolution that imbues microbes with new traits. Still another group is discovering ways to manipulate the essential biological circuitry of humans, using chemicals or engineered microbes to shut down defective genes or regulate the production of hormones controlling such functions as metabolism and mood.

Could a biowarfare weapons lab, such as Plum Island, have managed to create a new, weaponized version of Lymes disease that we are now calling Morgellons? Did they manage to genetically combine Lymes with a plant organism used in wastewater treatment to create a brand new disease? Is the population of the U.S. unwittingly acting as guinea pigs to this manmade sickness?

The symptoms of Morgellons, especially the fibers and feelings of bugs crawling and biting under the skin, are certainly odd and not what would be considered an effective biowarfare weapon. In biowarfare, the idea is to incapacitate, or even kill, the enemy so that they cannot resist an invading army. So far, Morgellons does not seem to be a fatal disease. However, as it progresses, its victims are left weak, helpless and possibly even contagious.

Maybe Morgellons is a new example of 21st century biowarfare, where instead of death; a population is rendered helpless with disease.

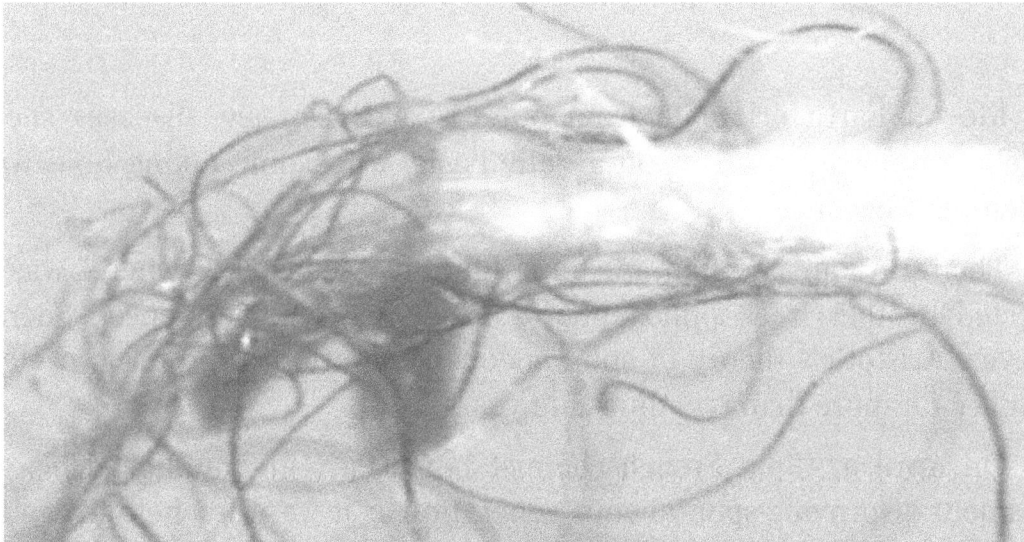

The strange threads of Morgellons could show a man-made connection.

CHAPTER FOUR

Is Morgellons From Outer Space?

DID life on Earth originate from outer space? Do new diseases such as Morgellons rain down on us on a daily basis, with some taking hold with a frightening vengeance?

The term Panspermian, meaning literally, "seeds everywhere" was first suggested by the Greek philosopher Anaxagoras, who influenced Socrates. However, Aristotle's theory of spontaneous generation came to be preferred by science for more than two thousand years.

On April 9, 1864, French chemist Louis Pasteur announced his great experiment disproving spontaneous generation as it was then held to occur. In the 1870s, British physicist Lord Kelvin and German physicist Hermann von Helmholtz reinforced Pasteur and argued that life could come from space. And in the first decade of the 1900s, Swedish chemist and Nobel laureate Svante Arrhenius theorized that bacterial spores propelled through space by light pressure were the seeds of life on Earth.

In the 1920s, Russian biochemist Alexander Oparin and English geneticist J.B.S. Haldane, writing independently, revived the doctrine of spontaneous generation in a more sophisticated form. In the new version, the spontaneous generation of life no longer happens on Earth, takes too long to observe in a laboratory, and has left no clues about its occurrence. Supporting this theory, in 1953, American chemists Stanley Miller and Harold Urey showed that some amino acids can be chemically produced from ammonia and methane. That experiment is now famous, and the Oparin - Haldane paradigm still prevails today.

Starting in the 1970s, British astronomers Fred Hoyle and Chandra Wickramasinghe rekindled interest in panspermia. By careful spectroscopic observation and analysis of light from distant stars they found new evidence, traces of life, in the intervening dust. They also proposed that comets, which are largely made of water-ice, carry bacterial life across galaxies and protect it from radiation damage along the way. One aspect of this research program, that interstellar dust and comets contain organic compounds, has been pursued by others as well. It is now universally accepted that space contains the "ingredients" of life. This development could be the first hint of a huge paradigm shift. But mainstream science has not accepted the hard core of modern panspermia, that whole cells seeded life on Earth.

Hoyle and Wickramasinghe also broadened or generalized panspermia to include a new understanding of evolution. While accepting the fact that life on Earth evolved over the course of about four billion years, they say that the genetic programs for higher evolution cannot be explained by random mutation and recombination among genes for single-celled organisms, even in that long a time: the programs must come from somewhere beyond Earth.

In a nutshell, their theory holds that all of life comes from space. It incorporates the original panspermia in the same way that General Relativity incorporates Special Relativity. Their expanded theory can well be termed "strong" panspermia.

LIFE ON EARTH

Most scientists have long assumed that life developed and evolved on Earth. According to the conventional hypothesis, the earliest living cells emerged as a result of chemical evolution on our planet billions of years ago in a process called abiogenesis.

The alternative possibility that living cells or their precursors arrived from space strikes many people as science fiction. Developments over the past decade, however, have given new credibility to the idea that Earth's biosphere could have arisen from an extra-terrestrial seed.

Planetary scientists have learned that early in its history, our solar system could have included many worlds with liquid water, the essential ingredient for life as we know it. Recent data from NASA's Mars Exploration Rovers corroborate previous suspicions that water has at least intermittently flowed on the Red Planet in the past.

It is not unreasonable to hypothesize that life existed on Mars long ago and perhaps continues there. Life may have also evolved on Europa, Jupiter's fourth-largest moon, which appears to possess liquid water under its icy surface. Saturn's biggest satellite, Titan, is rich in organic compounds; given the moon's frigid temperatures, it would be highly surprising to find living forms there, but they cannot be ruled out.

Life may have even gained a toehold on torrid Venus. The Venusian surface is probably too hot and under too much atmospheric pressure to be habitable, but the planet could conceivably support microbial life high in its atmosphere. And most likely, the surface conditions on Venus were not always so harsh.

Venus may have once been similar to early Earth. Moreover, the expanses of interplanetary space are not the forbidding barrier they once seemed. Over the past 20 years, scientists have determined that more than 30 meteorites found on Earth originally came from the Martian crust, based on the composition of gases trapped within some of the rocks.

Meanwhile, biologists have discovered organisms durable enough to survive at least a short journey inside such meteorites. Although no one is suggesting that these particular organisms actually made the trip, they serve as a proof of principle.

It is not implausible that life could have arisen on Mars and then come to Earth, or the reverse. Researchers are now intently studying the transport of biological materials between planets to get a better sense of whether it ever occurred. This effort may shed light on some of modern science's most compelling questions: Where and how did life originate? Are radically different forms of life possible? And how common is life in the universe?

In its modern form, the panspermia hypothesis addresses how biological material might have arrived on our planet, but not how life originated in the first place. No matter where it started, life had to arise from non-living matter.

The Final Nail In Your Coffin!

A biogenesis moved from the realm of philosophy to that of experimentation in the 1950s, when chemists Stanley L. Miller and Harold C. Urey of the University of Chicago demonstrated that amino acids and other molecules important to life could be generated from simple compounds believed to exist on early Earth. It is now thought that molecules of ribonucleic acid (RNA) could have also assembled from smaller compounds and played a vital role in the development of life. In present-day cells, specialized RNA molecules help to build proteins. Some RNAs act as messengers between the genes, which are made of deoxyribonucleic acid (DNA), and the ribosomes, the protein factories of the cell.

In the early stages of life's evolution, all the enzymes may have been RNAs, not proteins. Because RNA enzymes could have manufactured the first proteins without the need for preexisting protein enzymes to initiate the process, abiogenesis is not the chicken-and-egg problem that it was once thought to be.

A prebiotic system of RNAs and proteins could have gradually developed the ability to replicate its molecular parts, crudely at first, but then ever more efficiently. This new understanding of life's origins has transformed the scientific debate over panspermia. It is no longer an either or question of whether the first microbes arose on Earth or arrived from space.

In the chaotic early history of the solar system, our planet was subject to intense bombardment by meteorites containing simple organic compounds. The young Earth could have also received more complex molecules with enzymatic functions, molecules that were prebiotic but part of a system that was already well on its way to biology.

After landing in a suitable habitat on our planet, these molecules could have continued their evolution to living cells. In other words, an intermediate scenario is possible: life could have roots both on Earth and in space. But which steps in the development of life occurred where? And once life took hold, how far did it spread?

Scientists who study panspermia used to concentrate only on assessing the basic plausibility of the idea, but they have recently sought to estimate the probability that biological materials made the journey to Earth from other planets or moons. To begin their interplanetary trip, the materials would have to be ejected from their planet of origin into space by the impact of a comet or asteroid.

While traveling through space, the ejected rocks or dust particles would need to be captured by the gravity of another planet or moon, then decelerated enough to fall to the surface, passing through the atmosphere if one were present. Such transfers happen frequently throughout the solar system, although it is easier for ejected material to travel from bodies more distant from the sun to those closer in and easier for materials to end up on a more massive body. Indeed, dynamic simulations by University of British Columbia astrophysicist Brett Gladman suggest that the mass transferred from Earth to Mars is only a few percent of that delivered from Mars to Earth. For this reason, the most commonly discussed panspermia scenario involves the transport of microbes or their precursors from Mars to Earth.

IS MORGELLONS FROM MARS?

The symptoms of Morgellons certainly seem almost out of this world, creepy-crawly feelings under the skin, strange lesions that do not heal, and unusual thread-like material that exudes from the skin wounds. People from all over the globe are reporting the very same symptoms, and doctors are baffled.

What makes Morgellons so unique are the weird fibers that grow out of the victim's skin. No other disease known on Earth has this bizarre symptom. So could this mean that Morgellons could have originated somewhere other than Earth?

Mike Moore, who runs the website marslife.com, believes that this is the case and that Morgellons could have traveled to Earth on a meteorite.

But not just any meteorites, meteorites from Mars.

In the winter of 1970/71 Moore found a meteorite on a ranch in Texas. After careful study, Moore concluded that the unusual rock had formed under extremely dry conditions and was volcanic in origin. He believes that it came to Earth by the result of the impact of a large asteroid onto the surface of Mars.

"When I first found the meteorite, it had just come through our atmosphere, and the outer surface had probably been 'sterilized' by the high heat that melted the entire outer surface of the meteorite," Moore says. "It wasn't until 10 or 15 years later that I noticed that some 'fuzz' or 'filaments' were coming out of the crevice that runs through one side of the meteorite."

Moore was confused about what he was seeing. How could a rock from Mars be growing something that appeared to be alive? It was not until NASA announced in 1996 that they had found the possible remnants of life in a Martian meteorite that he began to consider that what he was seeing was some kind of Martian life growing on his meteorite. When he broke off a small sample of the meteorite, "sand" fell out.

Using a pocket microscope he found a piece of something that had obviously come from some kind of plant, or at least a living thing. It very obviously represented the remains of life of some kind and it had come from the meteorite. Attached to it was a filament. When he looked at it under the microscope and then looked at the fuzz coming out of the crevice, it seemed to Moore that they were the same "creature."

Moore spent several months at the Roswell UFO museum in New Mexico, where a worker offered to do some tests on the meteorite's contents. Moore gave him a small sample of sand that had fallen from the middle of the meteorite.

When the pile was examined under a microscope, it was apparent that the filament creatures were present in the sample. While trying to glue one end of one of the filament creature to a slide for study under the microscope, the filament moved back and forth, as if trying to avoid being stuck to the slide. Morgellons patients have also reported a similar movement of the "threads" and "fibers" that are associated with their disease.

Moore speculates that rocks blown off of Mars have been falling to Earth throughout history, bringing with them the minute life forms that we now call Morgellons. What still needs to be answered is whether or not Morgellons adapted itself to Earth conditions millions of years ago, or if it is a relatively "new" condition that has surfaced over the last few centuries.

There is also the feeling, according to Moore, that the Morgellons filaments almost seem intelligent. First, if one looks at their "constructions" one would have to think their behavior was deliberate.

"I often find them 'winding' along the walls of the vesicles of the rock. They have grown or moved to fit the walls of the vesicles and in the inner vesicles of the rock actually make 3D structures within the vesicles, extending from wall to wall and supporting structures in the middle."

It seems to Moore that they are collecting silicon: "It appears that tiny little panes of glass are being formed on the outside of the creatures."

Moore feels that the Morgellons creatures are not harmful and are in fact serving a good purpose by going after tiny insects that are already infesting their human host. However, nothing conclusive can be discovered until scientists accept the idea that Morgellons is real and does the proper research needed to find out once and for all if there is a connection between Morgellons and meteorites from the planet Mars.

RED RAIN OVER INDIA

Modern reports of Morgellons first surfaced in 2002. Strangely, Kerala, India may have had an extraterrestrial encounter in a mysterious red rain that fell in 2001.

Professor Godfrey Louis, at the School of Pure and Applied Physics of the Mahatma Gandhi University, said that: "Analyzing the red rain sample under an optical microscope, I found that it had cell appearances. Then I placed it under a transmission electron microscope and found that it had a detailed cell structure and a fine wall membrane."

Professor Louis, who published his findings in the **Astrophysics and Space Science**, Netherlands journal in November 2005, also noted that when he looked through a scanning electron microscope the sample showed the external morphology and it had a biological structure.

The professor found strange, thick-walled, red-tinted cell-like structures about 10 microns in size. Stranger still, dozens of his experiments suggest that the particles may lack DNA yet still reproduce plentifully, even in water superheated to nearly 600?F. (The known upper limit for life in water is about 250 degrees F.)

Louis speculates that the particles could be extraterrestrial bacteria adapted to the harsh conditions of space and that the microbes hitched a ride on a comet or meteorite that later broke apart in the upper atmosphere and mixed with rain clouds above India.

If his theory proves correct, the cells would be the first confirmed evidence of alien life and, as such, could yield tantalizing new clues to the origins of life on Earth. The story of the strange red rain began on July 25,

2001, when residents of Kerala, a state in southwestern India, started seeing scarlet rain in some areas.

"Almost the entire state, except for two northern districts, have reported these unusual rains over the past week," the BBC online reported on July 30. "Experts said the most likely reason was the presence of dust in the atmosphere which colors the water."

However, the explanation didn't satisfy everyone. The rain "is eluding explanations as the days go by," the newspaper *Indian Express* reported online a week later.

The article said the Centre for Earth Science Studies, based in Thiruvananthapuram, India, had discarded an initial hypothesis that a streaking meteor triggered the rain, in favor of the view that the particles were spores from a fungus. But "the exact species is yet to be identified. [And] how such a large quantity of spores could appear over a small region is as yet unknown," the paper quoted center director M. Baba as saying.

The red rain continued to appear sporadically for about two months, though most of it fell in the first 10 days. The striking red coloration turned out to come from microscopic, mixed-in red particles that had no similarity with usual desert dust.

It has been estimated that at least 55 tons of the particles have fallen in all. An analysis of this strange phenomenon further shows that the conventional atmospheric transport processes like dust storms etc. cannot explain it. Professor Louis speculates that a meteor may be responsible for the red particles.

The red rain phenomenon first started in Kerala after a meteor airburst event, which occurred on July 25, 2001 near Changanacherry in the Kottayam district. This meteor airburst is evidenced by a sonic boom heard by a number people during the early morning of that day.

"The first case of red rain occurred in this area few hours after the airburst. This points to a possible link between the meteor and red rain. If particle clouds are created in the atmosphere by the fragmentation and disintegration of a special kind of fragile cometary meteor that presumably contains a dense collection of red particles, then clouds of such particles can mix with the rain clouds to cause red rain," Professor Louis wrote.

It has been suggested that while approaching Earth at low angle, the meteor traveled southeast above Kerala with a final airburst above the Kottayam district. During its travel in the atmosphere it must have released several small fragments, which caused the deposition of cell clusters in the atmosphere.

Strangely, a test for DNA using Ethidium Bromide dye fluorescence technique indicates an absence of DNA in these cells. Nonetheless, Professor Louis wrote that the particles show "fine-structured membranes" under magnification, like normal cells.

"The major constituents of the red particles are carbon and oxygen," he wrote. "Silicon is most prominent among the minor constituents of the particles."

Chandra Wickramasinghe, director of the Cardiff Centre for Astrobiology at Cardiff University, U.K., thinks that a more careful examination of the red rain material is needed, but feels that at first glance, there is good evidence that the red rain could have extraterrestrial origins.

This is not the first time that Wickramasinghe has suggested that certain diseases may have their origins in outer space. Wickramasinghe and his colleagues suggest in a letter to the scientific journal *The Lancet* that the SARS virus may have arrived with 2,200 pounds of bacterial material that fall to the planet every day. That's 20,000 bacteria per square meter of the Earth's surface.

Some of this material is "highly evolved, with an evolutionary history closely related to life that exists on Earth," Wickramasinghe wrote in the letter. This, he wrote, "raises the possibility that pathogenic bacteria and viruses might also be introduced."

Epidemiologists, virologists, genomic researchers and other scientists worldwide have been working around the clock to track the origin of SARS and stem its spread. But if Wickramasinghe is correct in his space theory, their efforts may be moot.

"New cases might continue to appear until the stratospheric supply of the causative agent becomes exhausted," he wrote.

Medical history is rife with plagues and pestilences that could be attributed to space microbes, he said. He cited epidemics such as the plague of Athens, the plague of Justinian and the flu epidemic of 1918 as other outbreaks that could be space-induced, because they appeared and retreated abruptly.

"The patterns of spread of these diseases, as charted by historians, are often difficult to explain simply on the basis of endemic infective agents," he wrote.

He and his colleagues collected bacteria from a balloon launched from the Indian Space Research Organization and Tata Institute Balloon Facility in Hyderabad, India, on Jan. 21, 2001. This data showing how much bacteria entered the atmosphere from space led them to theorize that extraterrestrial disease-causing agents could affect the biosphere.

"A small amount of the culprit virus introduced into the stratosphere," he wrote, "could make a first tentative fall out east of the great mountain range of the Himalayas where the stratosphere is thinnest, followed by sporadic deposits in neighboring areas."

Matthew Genge, of the Department of Mineralogy at the London Natural History Museum, has estimated the amount of comet dust that survives entry into the lower atmosphere, and thus how frequently an average-sized human might be struck.

Genge figures that if you live to be 5,000 years old, you'll likely encounter one comet dust particle. Were it to harbor a virus, you would presumably have to inhale the particle, further reducing the odds of infection.

"Comet dust particles constantly rain from the skies -- around a hundred thousand billion particles per year -- and some of these will fall on people," Genge told space.com, adding that the extremely light particles would probably not be noticed. Genge said that some of the dust particles could contain bio-molecules.

LIVING ORGANISMS FOUND ON THE OUTSIDE OF SPACE STATION

In 2014, during a spacewalk intended to clean the International Space Station, Russian astronauts took samples from the exterior of the station for a routine analysis. The results of the experiment were quite surprising. Astronauts expected to find nothing more than contaminants created by the engines of incoming and outgoing spacecraft, but instead found that living organisms were clinging to outside of the ISS. The astronauts identified the organisms as sea plankton that likely originated from Earth, but the team couldn't find a concrete explanation as to how these organisms made it all the way up to the space station — or how they managed to survive.

Though NASA has so far been unable to confirm whether or not the Russians truly did discover sea plankton clinging to the exterior of the station, there is some precedent for certain creatures being able to survive the vacuum of space. Tardigrades, water-dwelling microscopic invertebrates, are known to be able to survive a host of harsh environments. They can survive extreme temperatures (slightly above absolute zero to far above boiling), amounts of radiation hundreds of times higher than the lethal dose for a human, pressure around six times more than found in the deepest parts of the ocean, and the vacuum of space. The organisms found on the ISS aren't tardigrades, but the little invertebrates show that some living organisms from Earth can indeed survive the harshness of space.

The bigger mystery is not that the plankton survived, but how they made it all the way up there, 205 miles above Earth. The scientists have already dismissed the possibility that the plankton were simply carried there on a spacecraft from Earth, as the plankton aren't from the region where any ISS module or craft would've taken off. The working theory is that atmospheric currents could be scooping up the organisms then carrying them all the way to the space station, though that would mean the currents could travel an astonishing 205 miles (330 km) above the planet.

There is the possibility that the "plankton" may have originated not from below the ISS, but from above. The idea that life exists all over the universe is known as Panspermia. This is the theory that life spreads across the known physical universe, hitchhiking on comets or meteorites. For example, life such as extremophiles, capable of surviving the inhospitable conditions of space, could become trapped in debris that is ejected into space after collisions between asteroids and planets that harbor life.

These life-forms may travel dormant for an extended amount of time before colliding randomly with other planets. The idea of directed panspermia, however, suggests that life forms are deliberately sent out through the universe by intelligent civilizations

Professor Francis Crick, one of the biologists who discovered the structure of DNA, examined the possibility of this in a paper in 1973. Professor

Crick and his colleagues did conclude that the scientific evidence was "inadequate at the present time to say anything about the probability."

However, since that time, other evidence that microscopic life may be raining down onto planet Earth from outer space has been uncovered.

MICROSCOPIC ORGANISMS FOUND IN UPPER ATMOSPHERE MAY BE FROM DEEP SPACE

Researchers from the University of Sheffield and Buckingham University claimed in 2013 to have found evidence for microscopic organisms living 16 miles up in the atmosphere. The scientists used a specially designed balloon to gather samples in the stratosphere during the Perseid meteor shower.

They found the fragments of single celled algae known as a diatom. They argue that this could be the first evidence to show how life may have arrived on Earth from space, perhaps carried here by meteorites.

Professor Milton Wainwright, from the department of molecular biology and biotechnology at the University of Sheffield who led the work, said: "Most people will assume that these biological particles must have just drifted up to the stratosphere from Earth.

"But it is generally accepted that a particle of the size found cannot be lifted from Earth to heights of, for example, 27km.

"The only known exception is by a violent volcanic eruption, none of which occurred within three years of the sampling trip.

"In the absence of a mechanism by which large particles like these can be transported to the stratosphere we can only conclude that the biological entities originated from space.

"Our conclusion then is that life is continually arriving to Earth from space, life is not restricted to this planet and it almost certainly did not originate here."

Also discovered in the samples was a tiny metal sphere that was oozing a "gooey" substance which Dr. Wainwright says could be an example of directed panspermia - where life was deliberately sent to Earth by some unknown extraterrestrial civilization. He argues that the strange material coming from the titanium ball, which is about the width of a human hair, is biological and could in fact be a colony of tiny microorganisms.

Dr. Wainwright said the sphere made a tiny "impact crater" on the sampler that was attached to the balloon as it collected dust and particles in the atmosphere.

He said: "This proves beyond doubt that the particle was travelling at speed from space when it was sampled."

Using X-ray analysis to examine the sphere, he concluded that it was made from titanium and traces of vanadium, while the material appearing to come out of the side was biological. They found that it also had a "fungus-like knitted mat-like covering."

Dr. Wainwright and his colleagues have published their findings in the Journal of Cosmology but their conclusions have yet to be corroborated by other scientists.

Professor Chandra Wickramasinghe, an astrobiologist at the University of Buckinghamshire and editor of the Journal of Cosmology who also worked with Dr. Wainwright on the study, added: "I think more work needs to be done on this particular structure, for example to study its DNA, if it has any.

"But already there is clear proof from many directions to confirm that we are constantly bombarded by fragments of comets that carry living microorganisms."

It is no stretch of the imagination then to suggest that Morgellons, as well as other unexplained and mysterious diseases may have arrived on Earth from the darkest regions of outer space. Considering how life is able to gain a foothold in some of the most inhospitable regions on the Earth, it is possible that the harsh realm of space is no barrier for life as it seeks to establish itself all across the universe.

CHAPTER FIVE

All in Their Heads

EVEN though sufferers of Morgellons display symptoms that are plainly apparent for all to see, most doctors refuse to believe that their patients are really suffering from a physiological illness. Instead, victims are often ignored or worst yet, told that their problems are psychological and not physical. If there is no insurance code into which the medical practitioner can "slot" a condition...it does not exist except as a delusional disorder.

Delusional parasitosis was first described in scientific detail and terms by Karl Ekbom, a Swedish neurologist, in 1937 and 1938. The form of delusional parasitosis described by Ekbom involves the conviction that parasites inhabit the skin, and this remains the most commonly encountered manifestation of the illness.

Those suffering from delusions of parasitosis believe that they are infected by parasites, insects and bugs. They report feelings of crawling bugs, stinging, biting or burrowing into the skin, and often causing itchy rashes and/or painful lesions that last for weeks or months and leave permanent scars.

Physicians distinguish between primary delusions of parasitosis, which occurs without any other underlying physical or mental disorder, and secondary delusions of parasitosis, which occurs as a result or symptom (or set of symptoms) of another condition, such as diabetes or schizophrenia. As unlikely as this condition seems, to doctors and entomologists, it is a reality. Ekbom said it was true. Since his article, physicians have essentially echoed him, without adding any scientific evidence to the theory.

Although some writers say that patients suffering from true delusional parasitosis exhibit no lesions on the skin, most acknowledge that they have seen the sores, rashes, and other evidence of an actual skin disease. Obvious bumps, rashes, etc., are sometimes explained as the result of "stress," acne, dry skin, contact dermatitis, or ordinary insect bites. However, sufferers are often described as having caused these skin problems themselves by excoriating or attempts at extermination or, as one source call it, self mutilation.

Some descriptions of this behavior are quite specific: "Excoriations are classically produced by the fingernails and there may also be signs of chemical burns as a result of attempts to kill the parasites. The patient is compelled to dig the parasites out, especially before going to bed, and often resorts to the use of a knife, tweezers or other sharp implement, leaving skin lesions consistent therewith."

Those that suffer from Morgellons have been told by their doctors that they had caused their own lesions even in places on their backs that they could not reach. Denying this behavior is pointless. "Self-excoriation is a common feature of delusory parasitosis, despite the individuals' protests that they do not scratch, doctors are quick to dismiss their patients complaints.

A circular logic is at work here. Attempting to remove parasites can only be evidence of being delusional if one already knows the parasites themselves are delusionary. A non-delusional individual truly infected by a skin parasite would behave in exactly the same way. It is only because the doctors have already decided that sufferers of Morgellons are delusional and that their behavior can be used to prove that they are delusional.

The single possible exception is scabies, and scabies does not really produce the same symptoms as Morgellons, and can be completely eradicated with one or two treatments with permethrin cream, a neurotoxin. If anything survives the treatment, it can't be scabies, the reasoning goes, and therefore must be a delusion.

MATCHBOX SIGN

Morgellons victim Jane Waldoch, a nurse for 24 year says she finds fibers that look like crunched up bugs in her sheets every morning. They come from the dozens of sores that cover her arms, legs, back and neck.

She began collecting samples of what was coming out of her skin. She thought it would help her doctors diagnose this bizarre and painful skin condition. She was wrong. Instead, Doctors took it as a sign that Jane was delusional.

"One of the hallmark clues to delusional parasitosis is what they call the matchbox sign. I guess in the older days people would take their samples in little match boxes to their physician," she says.

Mary Leitao, a biologist and the executive director of the Morgellons Research Foundation, said doctors have become "a brick wall. They have their answer, and they aren't open to discussing the possibility they could be wrong."

"They are so smug and sure they are right," she said.

Dr. Peter Lynch of the University of California, a dermatologist for 40 years, is one of the few skeptical experts who have been willing to even talk on the record. Others have ignored e-mails and telephone calls. He said "If there were a peer-reviewed study, with 15 or 20 patients who have the same exact thing in their skins, then maybe I'd believe it,"

"When fiberglass curtains first came out, many people with skin conditions were diagnosed with delusions of parasitosis (DOP), but studies showed these patients had tiny (fiberglass particles) in their skin."

Although it may seem perfectly reasonable for a person to bring a specimen for a doctor to examine, to do so with a skin disease turns out to be the most damning evidence of the patient's delusional condition. Called the "matchbox sign," or more recently by up-to-date dermatologists, the "Saran-wrap syndrome" or the "Ziploc sign," bringing in skin particles or materials found on or in the skin will carve the diagnosis of delusions into stone. Once again, perfectly normal behavior, based, in fact, on the "scientific method," becomes labeled as pathological.

A study conducted under the auspices of the National Pediculosis Association (NPA) in Needham, Mass., and the Oklahoma State Department of Health has found that ninety percent of patients with Morgellons were found to have Collembola, also known as Springtails, an almost microscopic insect with six legs, antennas, and no wings. Collembola feed on algae, fungi, bacteria and decaying matter.

The findings were reported in the edition of the *Journal of the New York Entomological Association*. The new findings bolster the contention of many patients that they "actually have something crawling on or under their skin and are not delusional," said the journal article.

INSECTS UNDER THE SKIN

Collembola predominately dwell in soil and litter, preferring wet or damp surroundings. They sometimes congregate in large numbers under leaky kitchen or bathroom sinks, swimming pools or in the soil of potted plants. Little is known about the health effects of Collembola, or how to prevent or treat them as a problem for human skin.

Lobelia Sharp, a plant pathologist at the University of California San Francisco, said she's had the lesions, fibers and other symptoms for about six months. When she sought medical help, she was diagnosed with delusional parasitosis, given antidepressants and taken by ambulance to the hospital and held in the mental ward.

She said she and a friend who is a mold scientist recently spent an evening using tweezers to snag "filaments" out of her skin welts and examine them under a microscope. The material – which she said was cellulose plant fibers – was similar to each other but unlike anything either of them had ever seen.

Dr. Noah Scheinfeld, from Columbia University, says Morgellons is not real. He says it's all in the patients head. Dr. Scheinfeld says, "This is somebody who is picking at themselves and people pick at themselves for all sorts of reasons." He says once patients create a sore they shove fibers into it.

Doctors such as Scheinfeld also say it's unlikely that the varied symptoms associated with Morgellons, from lesions to joint pain to loss of vision, could all be caused by the same disease. What's more likely is that as word of Morgellons spreads through the Internet and television news coverage, more people become convinced they have it. If this is the case, then Morgellons is one in a long line of weird diseases that have swept through populations, only to disappear without a trace once public concern subsides.

But Morgellons has not disappeared and a few doctors are now conducting the proper research to try and figure out the mystery once and for all. Beginning in early 2006, 14 Morgellons patients came to the lab of Randy Wymore, assistant professor of pharmacology at Oklahoma State University. Six are children and eight are adults. All have fibers that appear to be growing from their skin.

To prove that the fibers are not environmental contaminants, Wymore and his staff, which includes a doctor and a pediatrician, cut into the skin and remove colored fibers. "To find fibers underneath unbroken skin where there's no lesion, no scarring, no sign of scratching whatsoever, would preclude any possibility of this being contaminants from the environment," Wymore says.

He sends the fibers to an independent pathology lab in Tulsa. During the testing process the fibers are accidentally drained down a sink. He sent another batch in June and is still awaiting the results.

In the last few months, Wymore has been bombarded by phone calls and e-mails from Morgellons sufferers, family members and co-workers, even school principals who wonder if the disease is contagious. Doctors from all over the country have called, asking him how they should treat the disease. Since May, he has received 486 e-mails asking for some help or information. He wonders why the CDC isn't doing more.

"Why am I the one dealing with these people?" he asks. "I have no problem dealing with people in Oklahoma as a sort of public service aspect of my job, but when it starts coming from New York and California and Washington and Minnesota, I mean, we've crossed state lines, it seems to me this should become a federal issue."

THE CDC STUDY ON MORGELLONS

For those hoping that the Center for Disease Control would conduct a fair and unbiased study on Morgellons were in for a rude surprise. In 2008, at the request of California Sen. Dianne Feinstein, the CDC launched a study on Morgellons with a budget of only $360,000. According to the CDC, after performing detailed examinations of patients, running blood and urine tests, analyzing skin biopsies and "fiber" particles, conducting psychological examinations, and looking for disease clusters, the researchers could not find any common cause of illness among Morgellons patients.

They suggest that the patients' symptoms and histories are similar to those of patients with a psychiatric condition called delusional infestation -- the delusional belief that one is infested with parasites.

More broadly, the findings suggest that Morgellons disease may result from the downward mind/body spiral known as somatization or somatoform disorder. In these conditions, physical symptoms worsen underlying anxiety or mood disorders, which then worsens the physical symptoms.

The CDC claimed that they looked for patients treated from 2006 to 2008 for any Morgellons symptoms by Kaiser Permanente Northern California. Out of the 3.2 million people enrolled in the program, they identified 115 patients. Another 11 patients who heard of the study offered to participate. In the end, 41 patients had full physical examinations.

As in previous studies of Morgellons, the patients tended to be female (77%) and white (77%).

Three-fourths of the examined patients had sores on their skin. Half of the lesions were merely sun damage, but 40% showed signs of scratching or irritation, and 16% looked like bug bites or allergic reactions to drugs.

Sixteen of the lesions had materials stuck in them. Most turned out to be cotton fibers, probably from clothing; some were skin fragments likely caused by scratching. Importantly, normal areas of the patients' skin had nothing wrong with them, suggesting that there was no systemic skin disease.

Psychiatric evaluations showed that the patients' average intelligence was somewhat higher than normal. But 60% of the patients showed signs of cognitive impairment, and 63% had "somatic complaints," often "incapacitating fatigue."

According to CDC researcher Michele L. Pearson, MD, the patients' level of "functional impairment and disability" was "comparable to that detected among persons who have serious medical illnesses and concurrent psychiatric disorders."

To those who suffer from Morgellons, the CDC results came as no real surprise. Practically all had been told by doctors that they were suffering from psychiatric disorders and then routinely dismissed. However, for the doctors and scientists who had been conducting exhaustive research on Morgellons, and were convinced that it is more than just a mental disorder, the CDC study came as a professional slap to their collective faces.

A few closed shop and refused to have anything more to do with Morgellons research. While others were not going to be deterred from continuing to seek answers just because of one ill-funded government study. For the media, the Morgellons question had been answered; it was a case of Internet inspired mass-hysteria. Coverage on the subject practically disappeared. Nevertheless, during this period of informational near-vacuum, some amazing discoveries were taking place.

2015 – NEW PROGRESS IN MORGELLONS RESEARCH

In December of 2014, it was announced that research headed by UNH professor of biology and environmental sciences, Dr. Eva Sapi, Ph.D., successfully identified and confirmed that infectious organisms were present in Morgellons patient skin lesions. Evidence of two human pathogens, Borrelia burgdorferi and Helicobacter pylori, were identified by the analysis of whole genome sequencing. The goal of the next phase of Dr. Sapi's study is to provide more evidence that Morgellons disease has infectious agent etiology.

These discoveries are significant because they add further evidence that Morgellons is somehow connected to chronic Lyme disease. Dr. Ray Stricker, a Lyme-disease specialist, along with his colleague Marianne Middelveen, a veterinary microbiologist in Alberta, Canada, published a paper in 2011 (*"Filament formation associated with spirochetal infection: a comparative approach to Morgellons disease"*, 2011 Nov 14, Clinical, Cosmetic and Investigational Dermatology) noting similarities between Morgellons and a cattle skin condition called Bovine Digital Dermatitis.

Bovine digital dermatitis is an emerging infectious disease that causes lameness, decreased milk production, and weight loss in livestock. Proliferative stages of bovine digital dermatitis demonstrate keratin filament formation in skin above the hooves in affected animals. When they took samples from afflicted cows and humans with Morgellons, they found similar spiral-shaped spirochete bacteria; in people, it was the same bacterium that causes Lyme disease, Borrelia burgdorferi.

The hallmark of Morgellons disease is the mysterious fibers of unknown etiology that appear both in nonhealing or slow-healing skin lesions and beneath unbroken skin. The fibers resist extraction, and attempts to remove them may cause shooting pain. Patients with the affliction may experience crawling and stinging sensations from under their skin.

There is strong evidence that Morgellons is not a delusional disease. Fibers are found under unbroken skin, indicating that they are not self-inflicted. Because they are not self-implanted textile fibers, they must be produced within the skin. The lack of detectible pathogens in lesions suggests also that fibers are human cell products. Keratinocytes are the cells most likely to produce these fibers. They are the predominant cells found in skin, and they are found in hair follicles. Fibers have been found embedded in and piercing skin, and they have been observed growing out of hair follicles.

There is evolving evidence that Morgellons fibers have physical properties consistent with keratin. Keratin is a family of fibrous structural proteins and is the key structural material making up the outer layer of human skin. It is the key structural component of hair and nails, and it provides the necessary strength and toughness for masticatory organs, such as the tongue and the hard palate. Keratin and chitin are the strongest known biofibers, and keratin shows no cellular structure. Likewise Morgellons fibers are very strong and show no cellular structure, consistent with keratin filaments. They are colored blue, red, purple, and black, which are all colors found naturally in keratin.

Stricker believes Morgellons fibers are the body's reaction to chronic Lyme. "If you treat the underlying Lyme infection, you can make the body stop overproducing fibers." He treats his patients with long-term doses of antibiotics and claims to get positive results, though he acknowledges that in some cases it can take years for symptoms to ease.

CREATING PANIC IN THE GENERAL POPULATION

CIA informants have revealed that Morgellons could be a manmade disease that is being propagated by the secret elite group that controls the world through manipulation of war, money, wealth and poverty...the New World Order. Rumor has it that Morgellons is one of several diseases that have been released in order to create panic.

It currently appears that Morgellons is not, as such, a fatal disease, though some sufferers have committed suicide because of the maddening symptoms. However, the psychological impact of Morgellons is real and a serious concern. What remains unanswered is whether or not Morgellons is a naturally occurring disease that has suddenly emerged to infect humans, or if it is a manmade ailment produced as a terrorist or psychological weapon.

The Final Nail In Your Coffin!

Considering the current world situation, terrorist attacks, domestic spying, governments out of control and suppressing democracy and freedoms guaranteed by our founding fathers. It should come to no surprise that the New World Order could stoop to such evil as releasing a disease such as Morgellons upon an unsuspecting planet in order to create panic and chaos. Sometimes the smallest thing can cause the biggest problems. We have to take a deeper look, beyond the affliction itself, before we will find the answers – answers for which we are made to beg.

We cannot allow the truth about Morgellons to be swept under the rug with blanket dismissals of crazy and delusional. We fail in this task at our peril and with the ultimate cost of our health and lives.

Section Two

Red Mercury

CHAPTER SIX

Nuclear Secrets

THE CIA says it doesn't exist. Terrorists and rouge nations have offered to pay millions of dollars to procure it. Scientists fear its lethal potential.

Red Mercury - this ominous name has been long-whispered among the operatives in the nuclear underground and in the dark avenues of international espionage.

Red mercury is a compound containing mercury that has undergone massive irradiation. When exploded, it creates tremendous heat and pressure – the same type needed to trigger a fusion device such as a mini-neutron bomb.

Before, an obstacle to creating a nuclear bomb was the need for plutonium, which when exploded creates a fusion reaction in hydrogen atoms. But red mercury has changed that. The cheap substance has allegedly been produced in Russia and shipped on the black market throughout the world.

Do terrorist organizations now have red mercury neutron bombs? Some scientists say that with the help of red mercury, nuclear weapons of unimagined power could be contained in a package smaller than a softball and easily hidden in cities all over the world.

The potential is frighteningly real.

A man sits on a park bench across the street from the White House eating his lunch. He carries with him a brown paper bag - or perhaps even a lunch box. He keeps to himself. No one has any reason to pay any attention to him. Too bad they don't. After five or ten minutes, he gets up and walks away. He has left his "empty" bag behind. Five minutes later, there is a deafening explosion. A bomb has exploded that is so powerful – yet so small – that it kills everyone in the White House and most people within several yards in all directions.

The red mercury compound causes the neutrons to do the damage. They also blow out computers through electromagnetic pulsation. Because the bombs are so light and undetectable, these devices can be smuggled easily across the border hidden inside a coffee can.

The story is right out of a James Bond movie. The only thing is that the script writer is none other than Sam Cohen – the man who came up with the idea of the neutron bomb in the late 1950s. He will play an important part in our scenario.

Will the U.S. and other countries find themselves held hostage with nuclear terrorism by groups bent on total world domination with their iron-handed fundamentalist extremism? How can we prevent this and other potential terrorist threats from destroying the world as we know it?

WHAT IS RED MERCURY?

According to the article *Deadly Alchemy*, by Paul Sieveking, red mercury is an elusive substance said to be useful in nuclear weapons, medicine and voodoo. And interest in this enigmatic material can have deadly consequences.

Ian Kidger, 48, international sales director of British-owned Thor Chemicals, which imports mercury waste into South Africa for recycling, hung up the phone in early November 1991, told his wife he would be back shortly, and slipped out of his Johannesburg home. Several days later, he was found stuffed into the boot of his BMW sedan by two car thieves. His arms, legs, buttocks and head had been sawn off and covered in a black mercury compound.

As Thor Chemicals had long been accused of polluting the soil and ground water, his killing was initially blamed on eco-terrorists; then someone whispered the words red mercury and soon the South African press was off and running with its version of this intriguing mystery. The murder remains unsolved.

The Roman god Mercury not only presided over orators and merchants but also over thieves, pickpockets and villains of all stripes. He could make himself invisible or assume any shape he desired and gave early proof of his craftiness by robbing Neptune of his trident, Venus of her girdle, Mars of his sword, Jupiter of his scepter and Vulcan of many of his mechanical instruments.

How appropriate, then, that red mercury, a substance whose very existence is doubted by many Western scientists, should be touted by shady con men from Nairobi to Baghdad, fetching up to a million pounds a pint.

When the stuff first appeared on the international black market in 1977, the supposedly top secret nuclear material was "red" because it came from the Soviet Union; later, it actually took on a red color. A report from the U.S. Department of Energy, compiled by researchers at Los Alamos, entitled: *Red Mercury: Caveat Emptor*, began: "Take a bogus material, give it an enigmatic name, exaggerate its physical properties and intended uses, mix in some human greed and intrigue, and voila: one half-baked scam."

The report said that the wonder substance was offered as a modem philosopher's stone that can do just about anything: it makes stealth aircraft stealthier, infrared sensors more sensitive, counterfeits harder to detect, and atom bombs smaller and easier to build. Sometimes it is said to be radioactive, sometimes not. It might be the densest compound known to science, but then again, it might not.

All the samples recovered by official agencies – in countries as diverse as Ethiopia, North Korea and South Africa – had failed to have any special military application. They had included pure mercury, mercury tinged with brick dust, depleted nuclear reactor fuel, a mercury-antimony compound, mercuric iodide, mercuric oxide and mercuric cyanate.

The last mentioned was at least reddish and explosive, but had been used for decades in artillery shells. "There is a report of one lazy con artist trying to sell mercury in a bottle painted red with nail polish," noted the DOE. Noah Technologies Corporation, one of the largest suppliers of mercury chemicals in the United States, was telephoned in 1984 by someone claiming to be "Prince Shami, the financial minister of Nigeria." He said he needed red mercury liquid in order to color Nigerian money. He also needed it to stop fungus growth on this money. Bob Blumenthal of Noah Technologies met the Nigerian in Manhattan and tried to convince him that the substance didn't exist. But "Shami" insisted he wanted it and waved a very thick wad of high-denomination dollar bills around. Two weeks later, Blumenthal rang the Nigerian Embassy, but no one had heard of "Prince Shami."

Since then, Noah Technologies has received about five calls a month from people all over the world wanting to buy red mercury liquid for voodoo, medicine or nuclear business. In the mid 1980s, scores of prospectors rushed to West Pokot District in Kenya, where red mercury was allegedly "oozing from the hills." Official denials only strengthened popular belief.

According to one version of events, red mercury is an Antimony mercury oxide developed in the Soviet Union as a simple trigger for atom bombs. Such triggers, which surround a core of plutonium or enriched uranium, must be shaped so precisely that when exploded they uniformly compress the core, setting off a chain reaction; and they must provide an adequate supply of free neutrons to sustain that reaction. Red mercury supposedly combines both functions within one substance and enables the construction of bombs using smaller quantities of fissionable material than standard atomic warheads.

Small wonder, then, that Third World demand for red mercury is red hot – or that Russia's economic chaos has encouraged strenuous efforts to satisfy it. Such a substance could transform the regimes of Islamic terrorists into nuclear powers overnight. According to Evgeny Korolev, a politician in Ekaterinburg, a Russian center of red mercury trafficking: "With red mercury, a terrorist can make a bomb the size of a grenade that could blow a ship out of the sea."

The Final Nail In Your Coffin!

One American nuclear expert said that size was no longer important. NATO already possessed nuclear artillery shells and there were small, handy-sized nuclear mines.

THE NUCLEAR MENTALITY

For most of Sam Cohen's life, he has struggled against politicians who, in his opinion, have sacrificed good sense when it comes to the nation's defenses. Cohen is the physicist who invented the neutron bomb, the one that kills people but leaves things like tanks and buildings intact. Plans to deploy his creations in Europe during the 1970s and '80s awakened the "peace movement" across that continent, stopping its deployment.

With that and other battles lost, the elderly Cohen finds solace in his Brentwood home, nestled high on a hill overlooking Los Angeles. There the world is far more peaceful, or so it seems. Cohen would probably be unfazed if confronted by a knife-wielding mugger, a threat insignificant in the scheme of things. What worries him are weapons of mass destruction, nuclear ones that destroy whole cities.

The politicians tell us that our security has never been better. Cohen describes the present situation as "scary, scarier than ever before." He was concerned that the Bush administration had decided it was politically incorrect to even think about the design and development of nuclear weapons. The head of the division of the Livermore National Laboratories in charge of such weapon development has threatened to resign if he is ordered to develop new weapons, Cohen noted in an interview.

"The government doesn't want people to even think about nuclear weapons, which is like telling Sam Cohen he is no longer permitted to breathe."

As a kid from Brooklyn who graduated with a physics degree from UCLA, he enlisted in the Army after Pearl Harbor. In 1944 Cohen was assigned to the top-secret Manhattan Project to develop atomic weapons at Los Alamos, N.M. Cohen had the mundane job of calculating how neutrons behaved in "Fat Man" – the nickname of the bomb dropped on Nagasaki. (The bomb dropped on Hiroshima three days earlier was nicknamed "Little Boy.")

The boring work was all worthwhile because Cohen eventually stood in the Nevada desert and witnessed something on par with the Transfiguration: an atomic explosion. Cohen saw firsthand the awesome power of the unleashed atom as human history entered a new age. "Awesome spectacle" is how Cohen still described the event.

Puffing on a cigar as he relaxed in his easy chair wearing a T-shirt and jogging pants, Sam remembered that day vividly. "World War II flying hero Jimmy Doolittle stood next to me when the bomb went off. The little guy was blown down," Cohen recalled.

After the war ended, Cohen joined the Rand Corp. where he was paid to continue thinking about nuclear weapons. He was obsessed with the idea of a neutron bomb, one that would make use of the lethal particles he had observed so studiously at Los Alamos.

The earliest bombs had used nuclear fission, splitting heavy atoms to release energy. Later bombs used nuclear fusion, which fused hydrogen atoms to release energy. Both designs produced tremendous blasts that could level whole cities and left them uninhabitable for long periods because of lingering radiation.

Cohen's neutron bomb would use nuclear fusion, but in a different way. The detonation of a neutron bomb would still produce an explosion, but one much smaller than a standard nuclear weapons. The main effect of a neutron bomb would be the release of high-energy neutrons that would take lives far beyond the blast area. The result: fewer buildings, cars, tanks, roads, highways and other structures destroyed. And unlike standard nuclear bombs that leave long-term contamination of the soil and infrastructure, the neutron radiation quickly dissipates after the explosion.

For Cohen, the neutron bomb is the ultimate sane weapon. It kills humans, or as he puts it "the bad guys," but doesn't produce tremendous collateral damage on civilian populations and the infrastructure a civilian population needs to survive.

This meant, in Cohen's mind, that a conventional war could escalate without immediately leading to an all-out nuclear holocaust. If regular nuclear weapons were used across Europe, the radioactive fallout could turn the continent into a wasteland for decades. That wouldn't be the case if neutron bombs were used.

Between 1958 and 1961, the neutron bomb idea was tested successfully, but the politicians in Washington nixed development and deployment of the weapon. Cohen persisted. As the Vietnam War began and festered in the 1960s, Cohen became an advocate of using neutron bombs there. To Cohen, his weapon was "a perfect fit" for dealing with the Viet Cong hidden in the jungles and rice paddies.

Again, the politicians had other ideas. Secretary of Defense Robert McNamara ruled that no nuclear weapons of any type would be used in the war. The use of the small neutron bombs would have brought the war to a quick end, Cohen still argues, and saved the loss of more than 50,000 American lives. In 1969, Cohen was fired from the Rand Corp. for continuing to advocate the use of tactical neutron bombs to end the conflict. "I lost all my battles," Cohen said.

In 1979, he was in Paris helping the French build their own arsenal of neutron bombs when presidential candidate Ronald Reagan came through on a European tour. Cohen met with Reagan to brief him on the neutron bomb. Reagan grasped the idea of neutron weaponry immediately and made a pledge to Cohen, and later a public pledge, that he would reverse Carter administration policy by building and deploying a large number of neutron bombs.

As president, Reagan fulfilled that pledge and approximately a thousand weapons were constructed. But criticism from European allies kept the weapons from being deployed across Europe.

With the fall of the Berlin Wall and the end of communism as we knew it, the Bush administration moved to dismantle all of our tactical nuclear weapons, including the Reagan stockpile of neutron bombs. In Cohen's mind, America was brought back to Square One. Without tactical weapons like the neutron bomb, America would be left with two choices if an enemy was winning a conventional war: surrender, or unleash the holocaust of strategic nuclear weapons.

Other nations haven't been afflicted by the U.S. blindness regarding neutron bombs. According to Cohen, "Evidence exists that China has neutron bombs stockpiled, and that the United States gave the Chinese the technology to build them.

"Russia has a large quantity of such weapons, as well as the world's largest arsenal of nuclear weapons. Israel has hundreds of neutron weapons. The neutron bombs would allow Israel to stop advancing Arab armies and tank columns – even one on Israeli soil – without permanently contaminating the land.

"South Africa, which constructed a cache of neutron weapons before the end of white rule, claimed it dismantled those weapons before handing over power to the Nelson Mandela government."

Cohen, however, claims to have it on good authority that white military leaders still control the secret stockpile as "an insurance policy."

Most frightening for Cohen is the relative ease by which neutron bombs can be created with red mercury. Cohen says that red mercury is a compound containing mercury that has undergone massive irradiation. When exploded, it creates tremendous heat and pressure, the same type needed to trigger a fusion device such as a mini-neutron bomb.

To reiterate, before, an obstacle to creating a nuclear bomb was the need for plutonium, which when exploded could create a fusion reaction in hydrogen atoms. But red mercury has changed that. The cheap substance has been produced in Russia, Cohen said, and shipped on the black market throughout the world.

Cohen said that when U.N. inspectors went to Iraq to examine the Iraqis' nuclear weapons capabilities, the U.N. team found documents showing that they had purchased quantities of red mercury. The material means a neutron bomb can be built "the size of a baseball" but able to kill everyone within several square blocks.

The public isn't being warned about this development because the politicians have little desire to combat the menace or to confront nations like Iraq, Iran and Libya that likely would use such weapons, Cohen said.

Cohen has little faith in the politicians anyway. "Every president since Truman, with the possible exception of Eisenhower, would have sold the country out if it came down to a nuclear confrontation," he said.

IN THE HANDS OF TERRORISTS

Cohen was especially concerned that red mercury and other nuclear components could get into the hands of terrorists who could make the events of September 11, 2001, look pale in comparison. Countries of the former Soviet Union could be a rich source of such material for those willing to pay. Though the Cold War is over and Russia appears in disarray, Cohen suggested that the situation remains dangerous because Russia has "far and away substantially more nuclear weapons than we do." While U.S. policymakers have been busy dismantling our nuclear arsenal, Russia continues to modernize.

The United States has been paying billions of dollars for the leftover plutonium from Russia's dismantled weapons, but evidence indicates that the Russians have not been turning over weapons-grade plutonium. Instead, the United States has been paying for, and not objecting to, material from their nuclear power plants – a strong sign the Russians are not dismantling their weapons.

For decades, the specter of apocalyptic terrorism has lurked in the background, and experts have warned that someday some terrorist group would use weapons of mass destruction to wreak large scale death and mayhem. Witness such terrorist mega-events as the destruction of the World Trade Center, the Oklahoma City bombing and the Tokyo subway poison gas attack. All serve stark notice to the world's counterterrorism community that there is a potential for future terrorists to seek larger and more destructive weapons from the nuclear, chemical, and biological arsenals. But these weapons are closely guarded and well-protected.

At least that was true until the break-up of the Soviet Union. Its demise ushered in the rise of Russian organized crime and the smuggling of nuclear material, and it was only natural that something like red mercury would become a hot commodity in the international illicit arms trade. In fact, during the early 1990s, red mercury was so much in demand – and so little understood – that there were several creative scams pulled off by unscrupulous Eastern European agents against unwitting buyers. The Russians were relatively quiet about reports of illicit shipments of red mercury allegedly being smuggled out of their country. Some say that the Russians didn't want to admit that their nuclear security was ineffective. Others say that there were Russian mafia leaders close to then-President Boris Yeltsin and they were getting official cover for their red mercury dealings.

According to defense writers with Jane's publications in London, red mercury is much more than that. Produced in several military centers, including some in Kazakhstan, Russia manufactures about 60 kg a year, they say. Much of that is then placed on the black market by the Russian mafia, where it sells for about $300,000 a kilogram. Customers allegedly include Israel, Iran, Iraq, Libya, and Pakistan, and some of them may be employing Russian scientists to assist in making low-yield nuclear weapons.

From Russia come official denials, but they are often lukewarm in their sincerity. On the surface, the government maintains that red mercury is a scam orchestrated, according to one source, by "individuals close to the government and with the full backing of the security services."

At the bottom of it all, goes this line of reasoning, is an elaborate fraud to raise much-needed hard currency. Russian officials concede that their country's wealth of natural resources has attracted swindlers and con men of all stripes. They are better organized than ever, running sophisticated production and export networks and corrupting employees in state enterprises such as mines, shipyards and refineries. But Major General Vyacheslav Saltaganov, head of the Interior Ministry's economic crimes division, concludes that red mercury is only a get-rich scheme, saying that "our swindlers have managed to create a demand for it abroad."

The Czech Security Information Service of the Czech Republic boasts that one of their greatest successes was achieved by BIS intelligence officers in combating the proliferation of components, materials and technologies for the manufacture of mass destruction weapons, which ranks among the most serious global threats of today.

This well-known case culminated on Wednesday, December 14, 1994, when the detectives of the Criminal Police Headquarters seized in Prague almost 3 kg of uranium enriched with 87.7 per cent of isotope 235. The case is remarkable not only because it was the largest amount of U 235 ever seized in the world, but also in view of the excellent cooperation between BIS and the police.

The Final Nail In Your Coffin!

The two security agencies had first acquired certain information independently of each other, which they subsequently combined and proceeded jointly till a fast and successful police action. This operation won the Security Information Service extraordinary respect on the part of its Western colleagues and was even praised by President Bill Clinton. It heightened the credit of the Czech Republic as a country which can cope with the smuggling of strategic material.

According to BIS findings, most of the underhand offers of materials made in our country concern freely tradable metals and various radio nuclides which have no real importance from the viewpoint of nuclear proliferation. Investigation of particular cases often leads to identification of the targets' links to partners in countries of the former Soviet Union. An overwhelming majority of the recorded illegal offers of trade deals involving strategic nuclear materials are, however, attempts at fraud. For example, the one-time very frequent offers of the mysterious red mercury and osmium isotope Os-187 were obvious mystifications.

Materials which can be encountered on the Czech and foreign black markets with the highest frequency include sources of ionizing radiation Sr-90, Co-60 and Cs-137. Apart from the isotopes of strontium, cobalt and cesium, the traffickers also offer stolen tablets of moderately enriched uranium oxide – the so-called pellets of nuclear fuel for light-water reactors. The assortment further includes ionizing fire (smoke) detectors containing microgram amounts of plutonium, which non-experts believe to be saleable for enormously high prices.

Specialists looking into this peculiar trading are increasingly convinced that its true purpose is money-laundering, and pretended sale is just a popular form of legalizing illicit profits. Some of them indicate, too, that designations as osmium, lawrencium or red mercury may be cover names for other, perhaps really strategic materials.

The number of illegal trade deals believed to involve strategic substances significantly increased on a global scale in 1991-1992 and stayed at the reached level still in 1994. But according to the findings of both the police and the secret services, since 1995 it has been steadily declining because there is less of a demand for these goods.

CHAPTER SEVEN

Red Mercury: Fact or Fiction?

EVEN though authorities insist that red mercury does not exist, there is said to be an extensive smuggling network that stretches from the Urals through Romania and Bulgaria to Austria, Germany and Italy. In 1991, Bulgarian police seized beer-bottle-sized flasks of red mercury bearing Soviet military symbols.

In April 1992, Ukrainian police arrested thieves near the border attempting to smuggle out 80kg of the stuff. In Poland, eight kilos were found in a Lada car belonging to some Russians. Tass reported that two Armenians went to Siberia and kidnapped the son of a red mercury dealer to ensure delivery of their order. In November 1992, a Czech reporter said that he had become the first journalist in the world to buy red mercury on the black market...in Vladivostok. His assertion that it was used "mainly for the nuclear submarine program" was apparently a first in red mercury lore.

The Russian government seems schizophrenic on the issue. In August 1992, Security Ministry spokesman Andrei Chernenko reported to the media on the success of Operation Tral, designed to combat the illegal export of strategic raw materials.

He stated that red mercury "does not exist at all." Two months later, in another press conference, Chernenko said that "no major leaks" of red mercury had occurred. In December, Russian Vice President Alexander V. Rutskoi told the Seventh Congress of People's Deputies that the inventors of red mercury had obtained the necessary export documents and were selling it abroad in great quantities and at astronomical prices. He called for an urgent investigation, as had Valentin Stepankov, the Russian attorney-general, some time earlier.

In January 1993, the Security Ministry referred to the "phantom product" and predicted that "the search for the nonexistent substance has no prospects." It was possible that the export licenses referred to by Rutskoi were simply a cover for smuggling other precious materials such as uranium, plutonium, gold, osmium and iridium.

Ramaz Tadeyev is the scientific director of Alkor Technologies, a flourishing company in St. Petersburg that says it has developed the technology to make liquid red mercury.

"It can be used to make a nuclear weapon," he said categorically. "That is why the prices are so high."

Oleg Sadykov, president of Promecology, a large company based in Ekaterinburg and Moscow with official permission to sell red mercury, is equally certain about the potentially lethal nature of the substance. "The black market in red mercury for nuclear weapons is a real threat to all countries and Russia cannot stop it alone. The West needs to get organized."

A list of officially sanctioned red mercury export orders compiled for Russian deputies in Moscow records 30 separate applications. Companies in Germany, Britain, the US, Liechtenstein and Hungary are mentioned, but it has proved impossible to trace them. President Yeltsin, Premier Gaidar and atomic energy minister Mikhailov were all mentioned as having granted permission for export.

British nuclear weapons expert Frank Barnaby found the subject of red mercury far-fetched, but pointed out that quite a few senior Russian politicians, who were unlikely to be involved in a hoax, had claimed that the substance existed. He postulated a liquefied form of a mercury-antimony compound to which is added, in a reactor or particle accelerator, a transuranic actinide such as californium 252, "an extremely good emitter" of neutrons.

John Hassard, lecturer in nuclear physics at Imperial College, was also uncertain. He mused that antimony and mercury were both very heavy atoms which, when joined, created a lattice of "boxes" just about the size of plutonium atoms, "and that makes me think that you might be able to drift plutonium into it. Do that and you overcome, in one stroke, the problems of thermodynamics in the implosion of your nuclear weapon."

The South African Connection

Peter Hounam and Steve McQuillan, authors of **The Mini-Nuke Conspiracy**, told a news conference in Johannesburg, South Africa, that the government of former president F.W. de Klerk had "hoodwinked the world" by claiming to have destroyed all of South Africa's nuclear warheads. De Klerk said in 1993 that South Africa had made six warheads and all had been dismantled. Lola Patrick, spokeswoman for South Africa's Atomic Energy Corporation (AEC) commented: "It's absolute nonsense, absolute hogwash. They came to us with that story and we laughed at them. It's bull."

Hounam and McQuillan said unnamed sources had told them five nuclear weapons, including four high-technology neutron bombs, could be in the hands of right-wingers in South Africa opposed to the black majority government of President Nelson Mandela.

Asked how many devices he and McQuillan believed South Africa had produced, Hounam said: "We talk in the book about potentially 24; that's atomic weapons, thermonuclear weapons and so on. Then, on top of that, there were many hundreds built of small tactical nuclear shells – over 1,000. In terms of whether more (than six) weapons were built, there is no maybe.

"In terms of advanced nuclear weaponry being built, there is no maybe ... Where the maybes come in is whether the right wing has direct access to the weaponry. The circumstantial evidence is strong." Hounam said the shells, with a relatively small yield, were designed to be fired by the South African-developed long-range G-6 howitzer.

The authors said that South African scientists had developed a chemical similar to red mercury and that police have linked five murders in South Africa since 1991 to deals involving red mercury.

President Nelson Mandela shrugged off the claims that right-wingers could have access to nuclear weapons. Speaking before leaving for New York to attend the 50th anniversary celebrations of the United Nations, Mandela said: "We have been assured by those who are connected with this (nuclear) program that it was discontinued, that everything was dismantled and we have not the capability now for making weapons of destruction."

According to Edward V. Badolato and Dale Andrade, in their article for the *Fortean Times* (#69), South Africa became involved with red mercury because of its former covert nuclear weapons program and the ease with which various types of illegal weapons and material can be moved in and around southern Africa.

South African police consider the security of their border to be a major problem. Narcotics, drugs, counterfeit money, illegal arms and ammunition, elephant tusks, rhino horns and stolen vehicles are among South Africa's worst cross-border dilemmas, according to South Africa's National Crime Investigation Services.

The use of aircraft to smuggle illegal shipments is a daily occurrence all over Southern Africa, and the Russians are in the thick of this situation – both in providing transport aircraft and in the penetration of this area by the Russian mafia gangs.

For example, South African arms dealer Ters Ehlers, former private secretary to Prime Minister P.W. Botha, was implicated in unauthorized Namibia-to-Angola flights carrying illegal arms. Namibian Deputy Minister of Transport Klaus Dierks ordered a Russian An-12 transport plane grounded that was allegedly used to fly illegal supplies to Angola's UNITA guerrillas.

Ehlers has also been implicated in 1994 arms shipments to Rwanda's Hutu army which violated the UN arms embargo. There are four Russian An-12 transports for hire that are based at Lanseria airport near Johannesburg that are reportedly used for "special cargo missions." Lanseria Airport is considered to be one of Southern Africa's busiest and it is reportedly used frequently for smuggling operations.

There are also unconfirmed reports that the South African nuclear weapons program has developed, in addition to its admitted seven nuclear bombs, a nuclear artillery shell for the G5 howitzer and that red mercury played a role in the reduced-size nuclear charge designs. Additionally, it is well-known in South Africa that there are several Middle Eastern countries that are interested in purchasing these latest arms from dealers and arms companies, such as ARMSCOR, the manufacturer of the G5. Iranian arms shoppers are frequent visitors to South Africa, and some observers speculate that Hezbollah has sent shoppers to visit with some private arms dealers.

All this has been made even more sinister by four murders connected to red mercury. In 1991, there was the bizarre murder of Alan Kidger. Then, in April 1993, Wynand van Wyk, one of South Africa's top chemical engineers, was bludgeoned to death in a Cape Town hotel, where he had been lured to a false business meeting. He was believed to be providing Arab governments with chemicals to be used for military purposes. He had also had various business dealings with Kidger.

In July 1994, Dirk Stoffberg, an international arms trader, and his wife were found shot in their home in South Africa in what was termed a "murder suicide," but with suspicious evidence to the contrary. Stoffberg had been heavily involved in the Iran-Contra affair and he had been allegedly involved with red mercury.

Another big-time South African arms dealer, Don Lange, was found dead in June 1994 with his head in a plastic bag connected to a cyanide gas bottle. Officially ruled a suicide, there were strong indications that it could have been murder, a theory bolstered when South African officials quietly ordered a second autopsy on the body. Lange was involved with Kidger and had been heard talking about red mercury. Lange was also close to Gerald Bull, who had helped the South Africans develop their 155mm G5 Howitzer, one of the best artillery guns in the world. Bull was assassinated in Europe after his involvement in helping the Iraqis build their long range "Super Gun."

Police investigations and local reporters indicate that the four South African murders were linked by the victims' arms deals, nuclear and chemical weapons development expertise, Middle East contacts, and, coincidentally, interest in red mercury.

The Final Nail In Your Coffin!

There are several reasons why South Africa is an area of focus for those interested in red mercury. First, South Africa's police services are in a transition period and its crime fighting resources are stressed to the limit, allowing criminals to flock in to take advantage of illegal opportunities.

Second, similar to Russia, it is experiencing a "brain drain" of trained personnel from its nuclear weapons community as South Africa's Atomic Energy Corporation (AEC) budget has been severely cut from one billion Rand to 245 million Rand. The AEC says it is losing large numbers of nuclear scientists and engineers to foreign countries, with over 100 nuclear scientists and at least 500 nuclear engineers having departed over the past five years for greener pastures—possibly in technically advising on nuclear matters, such as red mercury.

Third, under South Africa's previous government, there existed a sophisticated international arms trading network, much of which remains intact among front companies and private individuals who know how to move special shipments and payments across national borders.

Fourth is the unofficial espionage network that has been a way of life, and old habits die hard for out-of-work intelligence agents. Recently, the Commissioner of the South African Police Services and other senior police officials discovered that someone was bugging their offices and phones. Meanwhile, South Africa's National Intelligence Agency was accused of spying on the Land Affairs Minister by placing a tracking device in the minister's official vehicle, for which the NIA denied responsibility. This is the type of situation that breeds intrigue and conspiracies – conducive to spreading the red mercury story.

Scientists Disagree

If red mercury is simply a fabrication from the minds of wily con men, then why do such noted scientists as Sam Cohen still insist that red mercury is very real and dangerous? Cohen has revealed that a powdered red mercury compound was first produced in 1968 at the E.I. du Pont de Nemours Company. When this compound was irradiated and pressured into a gel, the density substantially increased. This provided the necessary precondition for producing a neutron explosion.

However, in July of 1994, then-FBI Director Louis Freeh made the following statement regarding illegal black market sales of illicit nuclear materials: "Most were frauds where swindlers tried to sell harmless red mercury as more highly enriched radioactive material." Despite the denial of red mercury by Western governments, there are a growing number of weapon-hungry third world nations that are still attempting to procure red mercury.

During the 13th annual meeting of Doctors for Disaster Preparedness (DDP), which was held at Grants Pass, Oregon, attendees discussed the potential for various forms of natural disasters and terrorist attacks on the United States. During this discussion, controversy arose between Edward Teller, father of the hydrogen bomb, and Sam Cohen, inventor of the neutron bomb. The disagreement was over a narrow technical issue: the existence of red mercury.

As he had stated before, Sam Cohen insisted to his respected audience that there exists a new type of non-nuclear explosive that is potent enough to light off a nuclear fusion reaction between deuterium and tritium. In the usual H-bomb, a fission bomb is needed as a match to light off the fusion. With the new type of explosive, the fission bomb is unnecessary.

"As nuclear bombs go, the pure fusion bombs have an extremely low blast, equivalent to 1 ton of TNT: a 'pop, not a bang,'" according to Cohen. "But they release a flood of neutrons, lethal within 1/3 mile, causing death from immediately till shortly after."

The new types of non-nuclear explosives are called ballo-technic materials. Cohen says that unlike other explosives, they produce no bang, no cloud, keep the same shape while they detonate, "But boy, do they get hot!" Ballo-technics may have already led to very small fission bombs as well as pure fusion.

Cohen identifies the mysterious red mercury as a ballo-technic material. He offers this recipe: take mercury-antimony oxide, compress it and bombard with neutrons. He says it is slightly radioactive, with a half-life of a couple of days.

Cohen says the Russians have built and tested mini-nukes, and that Americans and Russians are cooperating on pure fusion. He says that a Russian bomb was brought to Los Alamos ("by Federal Express" from a

Russian plane in Washington) and successfully tested. Ballo-technics' potential for good is also great: it could be a route to practical fusion power.

Dr. Teller agreed with most of this – including the successful test at Los Alamos – but rejected red mercury as "nonsense," possibly "a pure hoax."

Russian Involvement in the Production of Red Mercury

Historically, the Russians have been leaders in high-pressure technology which is very relevant to the production of red mercury. In 1991, a Russian company called Promekologia, headed by Boris Yeltsin's ecological adviser, was granted a license to develop and exploit the country's advances in weapons and energy. In February 1992, Yeltsin signed Secret Directive No. 75-RPS, which authorized the company to manufacture and sell red mercury in amounts up to ten tons per year.

In 1993, Russian General Y. Negin claimed his country had developed a low-yield nuclear weapon "in which a doubling of yield is achieved with a hundredfold reduction of weight compared to existing weapons." A Russian official named Evgeny Kerolev said that red mercury is so potent that a "bomb the size of a grenade could blow a ship out of the sea." Russian Minister of Atomic Energy, Victor Mikhailov, said: "You can drop a couple hundred little bombs on foreign territory and the enemy is devastated."

In an article which appeared in the Russian newspaper, *Pravda*, Mikhailov said that these "little bombs" were micro-neutron bombs designed to wipe out people while leaving buildings standing. Mikhailov did not admit that Russia had actually developed such a weapon but he did say that "such a weapon could appear by the year 2000."

Russia was not alone in the secret development of low-yield weapons. In 1961, the U.S. tried to develop a low-yield pure fusion weapon at the Lawrence Livermore laboratories. The Los Alamos lab was involved in a similar project back in the early 1970s, but neither project produced a workable weapon. Such a weapon would be very inexpensive because it would not require uranium or plutonium. It would only require small amounts of tritium.

Dealing with this potential for nuclear terrorism should be one of this nation's highest national priorities, but U.S. government officials and agencies deny the potential existence of the micro-neutron bomb. The U.S. position of denying the technical feasibility of such a weapon could prove to be disastrous to our national security. This is not the first time that the government and the scientific community said a bomb was impossible to build. In the late 1940s, they said the hydrogen bomb couldn't be built, but shortly thereafter the Soviets deployed a hydrogen bomb.

Is there any validity to the red mercury stories? Alleged samples of red mercury have been sent to the U.S. Department of Energy's nuclear labs on various occasions, but so far, according to lab sources, the red mercury tests have all turned out to be fake. One similar chemical that may be adding to the confusion is fulminate of mercury, which bears a resemblance to the red mercury descriptions of an ocher-colored substance. But fulminate of mercury has no nuclear applications and is not radioactive. It is a poisonous substance that is frequently used in small explosives, such as shotgun cartridges, and it was known to be used years ago in rocket propulsion systems.

The bottom line is that there is no official confirmation of the existence of red mercury. In Great Britain, the standard denial is that "there is no evidence that red mercury exists." The US Department of Energy says that "the alleged samples it has been asked to test were worthless" and that it doubts "if red mercury really exists."

Vic Hogsett, an analyst at the Los Alamos nuclear research facility, said, "This is the unicorn of modern science. You can put your hand on a Kalashnikov, you can touch plutonium. With red mercury, there just doesn't seem to be anything there. Call it red mercury, call it a Big Mac. I call it a scam."

On the other hand, the prestigious International Defense Review in 1994 chastised Western governments for dismissing red mercury without more detailed tests. The outright denials, the article argued, raise the possibility that "red mercury is already taken seriously by many governments and that public pronouncements of the substance as a hoax serve merely to divert attention."

An interesting development on the verification of the reality of mini-neutron nuclear weapons came in 1993 when the United States Congress passed a bill banning research and development of micro bombs with yields less than five kilotons. Whatever the case, the terrorism angle is impossible to ignore. If red mercury exists in some form and does even a fraction of what some experts say it can, then it would be a very attractive package for any group interested in expanding into the field of nuclear terrorism. What is needed is a detailed investigation and explanation of the actual level of the threat so that the issue of red mercury can either be put to rest or given the counterterrorism priority it deserves.

Is there any proof that red mercury actually exists?

CHAPTER EIGHT

Seeds of Destruction: Bioterrorism

THEY came as simple letters. All over the planet they sat in mailboxes, small time bombs of unimaginable destruction, silently waiting for some unsuspecting soul to release their deadly contents. Contents that while invisible to the naked eye carried with them the potential of painful sickness and eventual death. God's smallest creations, now used as weapons of annihilation by terrorists against their enemies...weapons of the apocalypse that cannot be detected until it is too late and the fatal damage is done.

In the last century, terrorists used violence to try to get power or approval. Nowadays, those who feel marginalized within the world economy, from religious extremists to the merely unhinged, increasingly just want to kill people or damage industries. So far they have struck mainly with guns, bombs, and most recently, hijacked commercial jetliners. But the perfect weapon for those who wish only to kill or destroy is germ warfare – and we might have little defense.

With the ever growing fear that terrorists may try to attack using germs or deadly chemicals, governments around the world are urgently reviewing their counter-terrorist measures. One of their biggest unknowns is whether terrorists are now likely to stick to the low-tech approach of September 11, 2001, or whether they will turn to chemical or biological weapons.

The question is urgent because vast amounts of government money worldwide are soon likely to be channeled towards developing better counter-terrorism approaches. Attacks like those on New York and Washington D.C. are based on undermining the infrastructure of urban society, and the measures needed to guard against these are largely unexplored. Until the attacks on the U.S., virtually every analysis of the terrorist threat, and much counter-terrorism funding, assumed the enemy would use chemical, biological or nuclear weapons.

Terrorism experts are now calling for a wider-ranging risk assessment. "We focused on where we were most vulnerable, not on what kind of attack was most likely," says John Parachini of the Monterey Institute of International Studies in an interview for *New Scientist* magazine. "Chemical or biological attacks have high consequences, but low probability."

But experts also warn that, as we boost our defenses against hijacking, terrorists will seek other weapons. Terrorism experts are now warning that chemical and biological threats cannot be discounted.

Four factors were thought to discourage chemical or biological terrorism, says Rohan Gunaratna of the Centre for the Study of Terrorism and Political Violence at St. Andrew's University in Scotland. Three are now shattered: the historical reluctance of terrorists to kill many people, to remain anonymous – it can be hard to claim credit for an epidemic – or to use suicide weapons.

The only factor remaining now is technical difficulty. Amy Smithson, of the Stimson Center in Washington, thinks terrorists are highly unlikely to use germs or chemicals when explosions and the like are easier. However, events in the United States with anthrax-containing letters indicate that individuals or terrorists have managed to get hold of weapons-grade anthrax bacteria. The source of this highly refined disease is open to speculation, but only several countries have produced such germs. Yet the Soviets, Iraq, and the Japanese Aum Shinrikyo cult are known to have produced germ and chemical weapons in the recent past. Russia still guards tons of old Soviet weapons – which could still be redeployed by the likes of terrorists or even President Vladimir Putin.

The analysis is made yet more difficult by suspicions that officials will continue to warn of chemical and biological threats simply because they always have. Firms or researchers working on chemical and biological defense may also be reluctant to see the threat fade. Governments now deciding how to apportion their counter-terrorism budgets will have to assess whether these warnings are scare stories – or something they will one day wish they had heeded.

Russian Expert says "U.S. Not Ready For Bioterrorism!"

Is the U.S. unprepared for an attack with biological weapons? Ken Alibek thinks so. He has a unique perspective. In 1992, he blew the whistle on the Soviet Union's Biopreparat bio-warfare machine. The program was one of the great deceptions of the Cold War because the Soviet Union had signed a treaty banning such work. At its height, Biopreparat employed 10,000 scientists at 40 sites. Kanatjan Alibekov (Alibek's birth name) was second in command at Biopreparat, so his defection made him a fabulous prize for the U.S. Now he's a key researcher at a major U.S. biodefense contractor.

Alibek says that, in the 20th century, countries interested in biological weapons mostly developed them as weapons of mass destruction, a means to conduct wars. In the 21st century, we will see a significant shift.

"Everything is going to be done covertly. In some cases, biological weapons will be used in so-called 'low intensity' military conflicts, or they will be used [for terrorism], brought to the US and used to infect people in the subway, for example. You can criticize Putin or Yeltsin, but they are not stupid. They won't deploy biological weapons against Western countries.

"Russia still retains this huge, sophisticated biological weapons capability and expertise. This is the actual threat: not from the government, but from Russians with the knowledge. Some of them want to sell their expertise and knowledge. There are many buyers. My major concern is that in the event of a bioterrorist attack with well-trained people who know how to deploy biological weapons, the number of casualties would be unbelievably huge."

Alibek, who now resides in the United States, says that he now works to help protect people from the terrors of germ warfare.

The Final Nail In Your Coffin!

"Our approach at Advanced Biosystems is significantly different. There are two subsystems of the immune system: acquired immunity, which is activated by vaccines against specific antigens, and innate immunity, which works non-specifically. We are targeting innate immunity, which is theoretically capable of protecting against any infectious agent. The project is funded by the U.S. Army."

Biological weapons work mostly by infecting people through their respiratory tract. Advanced Biosystems is now working on ways to enhance innate immunity in the respiratory tract. Scientists have identified a group of cytokines capable of activating the immune cells of the respiratory tract. Their objective is to develop an inhaler containing micro-encapsulated cytokines to prevent degradation and toxicity. The inhaler could be used to treat people before a biological weapons attack and after they are exposed. The company believes that this approach could reduce casualty numbers significantly in the event of a biological attack, and it could also be used to protect against some naturally occurring respiratory infections such as influenza or tuberculosis. With government approval, these products could be ready for mass-production in less than a year.

Alibek says that all countries need to take a very aggressive approach and start developing real protection against biological weapons. In the United States, a special government board is needed that oversees this work, which covers everything from detection, identification, protective garments and disinfection, to the organizational tactics of medical services, diagnostics issues, treatment, re- treatment, and urgent prophylaxis.

Bioterror Trial Run

Aum Shinrikyo, the Japanese doomsday sect that killed 12 people by releasing sarin nerve gas into the Tokyo subway in 1996, had the knowledge and skills to wreak even greater devastation with anthrax. New research in the U.S. shows that Aum not only had the ability to release anthrax, it even did so, though it used a non-virulent strain.

The sect cultured the bacteria in large drums of liquid in the basement of its eight-story headquarters in the Tokyo suburb of Kameido, says Hiroshi Takahashi of Japan's National Institute of Infectious Diseases.

Then, in July 1993, Aum members pumped the liquid to the roof and sprayed it into the air for 24 hours.

The police investigated when neighbors complained about the smell, but Japan's religious protection laws prevented them from searching the building. But they did manage to take samples of a fluid leaking from a pipe on the outside of the building.

Medical records show that no one reported any anthrax symptoms in the area after the spraying, Takahashi told an anthrax conference in Annapolis, Maryland. The fact that Aum was unable to infect people with anthrax is cited by many terrorism experts as evidence that bioweapons are too complex for such extremists.

But scientists at Northern Arizona University in Flagstaff analyzed the fluid sample and found it contains plenty of healthy anthrax bacilli. DNA analysis shows they belong to the Sterne strain, which is used in live anthrax vaccines for animals. Sterne anthrax lacks a fragment of DNA necessary for the bacteria to cause disease and is easily purchased in the vaccine form. "It wouldn't have made anyone sick," says Timothy Smith, a member of the team.

Why would terrorists spray harmless bacteria? They may have been practicing, says Smith. Police attention could have discouraged them from moving on to virulent bacteria. Worryingly, the results show that Aum had got around the main difficulties with bioweapons – dead cultures and inadequate spraying. "I have no doubt people would have been sick, and probably died, if they had used a virulent strain," says Smith.

"Most terrorists still prefer explosives or arson," says David Claridge, a terrorism specialist at Rubicon, a security consultancy in London. One of the few exceptions, he fears, might be people committing hate crimes.

Scientist's worldwide are on the alert for lab accidents that could inadvertently create an even more lethal bug with potential terrorist applications. A virus that kills every one of its victims by wiping out part of their immune system has already been accidentally created by an Australian research team. The virus, a modified mouse-pox, does not affect humans but it is closely related to smallpox, raising fears that the technology could be used in bio-warfare. The discovery highlights a growing problem.

The Final Nail In Your Coffin!

How do you stop terrorists taking legitimate research and adapting it for their own nefarious purposes?

The Australian researchers had no intention of producing a killer virus. They were merely trying to make a mouse contraceptive vaccine for pest control. "But it's a good way to show how to alter smallpox to make it more virulent," says Ken Alibek, former second-in-command of the civilian branch of the Soviet germ-warfare program.

Ron Jackson of CSIRO's wildlife division and Ian Ramshaw at the Australian National University, both in Canberra, inserted into a mouse-pox virus a gene that creates large amounts of interleukin 4. IL-4 is a molecule that occurs naturally in the body. As part of a study aimed at creating a contraceptive vaccine, they were trying to stimulate antibodies against mouse eggs, which would make the animals infertile. The mouse-pox virus was merely a vehicle for transporting the egg proteins into mice to trigger an antibody response. The researchers added the gene for IL-4 to boost antibody production. The surprise was that it totally suppressed the "cell-mediated response" – the arm of the immune system that combats viral infection.

Mouse-pox normally causes only mild symptoms in the type of mice used in the study, but, with the IL-4 gene added, it wiped out all the animals in nine days. "It would be safe to assume that if some idiot did put human IL-4 into human smallpox they'd increase the lethality quite dramatically," says Jackson. "Seeing the consequences of what happened in the mice, I wouldn't be the one who'd want to do the experiment."

To make matters worse, the engineered virus also appears unnaturally resistant to attempts to vaccinate the mice. A vaccine that would normally protect mouse strains that are susceptible to the virus only worked in half the mice exposed to the killer version. "It's surprising how very, very bad the virus is," says Ann Hill, a vaccine researcher from Oregon Health Sciences University in Portland. Is it possible that research into new vaccines against cancer and other diseases could inadvertently create lethal human viruses? Many of the most promising modern vaccines depend on viruses to transport genes into the body and contain genes that directly alter the immune response. But researchers have not been too concerned because the evidence until now suggested that changes in the genetic make-up of viruses invariably makes them less virulent, not more.

One way to reduce the risk, says Gary Nabel of the National Institutes of Health, is to use only viruses that cannot replicate. "There are some replication-competent [viral vaccines] around, but there is increasing concern about their use," he says.

Defense experts are also worried about preserving the freedom to publish medical findings while trying to stop the information falling into the wrong hands. According to D. A. Henderson, a former U.S. presidential adviser and director of the Center for Civilian Biodefense Studies at Johns Hopkins University in Baltimore, what are effectively blueprints for making microorganisms more harmful regularly appear in unclassified journals. "I can't for the life of me figure out how we are going to deal with this," he says.

The Australian researchers consulted their country's Department of Defense before submitting the work for publication and only decided to go ahead after considerable thought. A report appeared in the February, 2001, issue of the *Journal of Virology.*

"We wanted to warn the general population that this potentially dangerous technology is available," says Jackson. "We wanted to make it clear to the scientific community that they should be careful, that it is not too difficult to create severe organisms."

However, meatball shaped molecules studded with molecular bait could mop up viruses before they get a chance to attack cells. Such "nano decoys" could filter out biological weapons in gas masks or even intercept viral invaders when injected into people.

In the past, researchers have tried to make decoys with long chain-like molecules. But controlling the length of these molecules has proved to be difficult, and it's hard to get rid of stray "links," or monomers, which are toxic. Replacing the linear polymers with molecules called dendrimers may be the answer. Because of their round shape, dendrimers may foist more receptors on to a virus than the linear polymers.

Fear of Bioterrorism Spreads Across the Globe

As more and more cases of anthrax are being reported, panic across the planet continues to grow as suspicious letters and packages are examined more closely for potentially deadly contents. Jets are rerouted and forced to sit on runways for hours after flight crews find unidentified white powder in the overhead compartments. Stores are quickly emptied when powder of unknown origin is found in the rest rooms. Family planning clinics are closed down as right-wing domestic terrorists take advantage of the situation and threaten women patients with death from anthrax.

Around the world, nations were reporting false or pending anthrax cases, and many were taking precautions after people in the United States were either infected or exposed to anthrax. For example, dozens of government workers in Australia took decontaminating showers after their office received a letter containing white powder, and a U.S. consulate was evacuated in a similar scare. Both turned out to be hoaxes.

A white powder was found in the mailroom at German Chancellor Gerhard Schroeder's offices, and authorities were investigating whether the substance is dangerous, the government said. Gas masks were selling briskly in Hong Kong, China has ordered new quarantine checks on suspicious mail from abroad and Australia is considering protective gear for postal workers.

Several anthrax and bomb scares were reported in Australia, where Prime Minister John Howard has come out staunchly behind the U.S.-led airstrikes on Afghanistan. Howard said that all anthrax scares so far had proven to be hoaxes.

In October 2001, authorities evacuated both the U.S. Consulate in the southern Australian city of Melbourne and the offices of the *Melbourne Herald and Weekly Times* newspapers after letters containing suspicious chemicals were delivered. U.S. Consul-General David Lyon said 40 staff were evacuated from the consulate as a precaution after an envelope containing a mysterious residue was hand-delivered by a person "in a great rush."

A police spokesman said the package was found to be harmless. Evacuated staff returned to work about 45 minutes later. Health authorities also ordered two floors of the Herald and Weekly Times building evacuated and a section of a road nearby cordoned off after five suspicious letters were delivered, one containing powder, a police spokesman said. Seventeen workers underwent decontamination, but no one was suffering any effects from exposure to the substance, the spokesman said on condition of anonymity.

In the Queensland state capital, Brisbane, six suspect parcels with the names of President Bush and Microsoft boss Bill Gates were delivered to various addresses. The police commissioner, Bob Atkinson, said the packages did not contain any powder.

But fear of terrorism using anthrax in the United States has become a deadly reality. Envelopes carrying anthrax in the form of a powder were sent to government officials and news organizations. The Central Asian nation of Kazakhstan, site of Soviet-era anthrax production, denied any involvement in the anthrax cases discovered in the United States.

The plant at the remote steppe settlement of Stepnogorsk was built starting in 1982 to replace another Soviet factory in Russia's Ural Mountains that accidentally released anthrax into the air in 1979, killing about 70 people. The huge facility was just one of six in the former Soviet Union, which had the largest biological weapons complex in the world.

In China, new quarantine checks of express mail from abroad were ordered, but an official said the screening was unrelated to the September attacks. Japan has tightened postal checks and has urged its citizens to report suspicious mail to police. Post offices were using X-rays to screen all international mail and parcels that have no return addresses. Workers at the Tokyo Central Post Office wore white masks Monday when handling mail and parcels.

An international airport terminal in Vienna, the Austrian capital, was closed for awhile after a passenger reported finding suspicious powder in a newsstand, which was tested negative for anthrax.

Several hundred people were evacuated from Canterbury Cathedral in England after a worker said he saw a man dropping white powder in one of the chapels. The historical cathedral, also a popular tourist spot, was reopened after police said tests found no traces of harmful substances in the powder.

The fear that madmen could be using anthrax as a medium of terror has become more significant since October 4, 2001, when a photo editor for the tabloid newspaper The Sun died of anthrax after being exposed to the disease from an anonymous letter. Seven other employees of American Media Inc. tested positive for exposure and were treated with antibiotics. None developed the disease.

Other news media outlets, leading politicians and a Microsoft office in Nevada were also targeted for the unexplained anthrax-containing letters. NBC news anchorman Tom Brokaw was the recipient of one such letter that was opened by a personal assistant. Erin O'Connor was exposed when she opened a letter containing a brown granular substance, which was mailed to Brokaw from Trenton, N.J. It was postmarked September 18, one week after terrorist attacks on the World Trade Center and Pentagon.

On October 15, 2001, a package that tested positive for the deadly bacteria was opened at the Washington office of Sen. Majority Leader Tom Daschle. The office was immediately quarantined and closed. Over 40 staffers were examined and treated. FBI sources said that the package was postmarked Trenton, New Jersey, the same postmark as a letter containing anthrax that was sent to Tom Brokaw.

In Nevada, a letter was sent to a Microsoft office in Reno that contained pornographic pictures contaminated with anthrax. Health officials said tests of four people who may have been exposed proved negative for the bacteria.

At first, federal authorities had stated the anthrax contained in the suspect letters was "low-grade" in quality and didn't appear to be "enhanced" by laboratory assistance. However, that all changed on October 15 when Senate Leader Tom Daschle received a letter containing a suspicious powder. Twenty staff members tested positive for exposure to anthrax. Tests confirmed that the letter was found to contain a highly refined form of anthrax, suggesting it was produced by experts.

One of the nation's leading biological warfare researchers said that the appearance of multiple anthrax infections suggests the possibility of a bioterrorist attack.

"The level of suspicion is high for me, though it's still open for me whether it's a bioterrorist attack," said C.J. Peters, former chief of special pathogens at the CDC.

Peters, now a professor of microbiology and coauthor of the 1997 book "Virus Hunter," said his suspicion may turn to certainty if strains of the bacteria found in Florida, New York, Nevada and Washington D.C. are the same. "If so, then there is one bad guy or one bad organization out there doing this," he said.

A federal official familiar with the investigation said that, prior to the New York exposures, investigators were treating the Boca Raton incident as an "isolated criminal case." But with the New York and Nevada cases, the same official shifted gears: "Maybe there is a concerted conspiracy connected to the Sept. 11 attacks."

Frederick Southwick, chief of infectious diseases at the University of Florida, said investigators seeking to link the Florida and New York anthrax events must find the same bacteria strain to make the link.

"The key is whether the DNA fingerprint of the strain in New York matches the DNA fingerprint of the one in Florida," he said. "If it matches, then one person or one organization is perpetrating this thing. If it doesn't match, then New York could be a copycat incident."

In South Florida, a potential link between the terrorists and anthrax cases involves hijacking suspect Ahmed Alghamdi. Using the Internet and an address in Saudi Arabia, he subscribed to Mira, the Spanish-language tabloid published by American Media Inc., according to law enforcement sources.

It is one of two tabloid subscriptions now under scrutiny by federal investigators, who said they intend to scour the tabloid giant's databases to see whether classified ads were used by the hijackers to communicate with other terrorist cells.

Even though alarm over anthrax infection is spreading, to be actually contaminated with anthrax to the point of infection is not an easy thing to happen. Anthrax is a bacterium that may cause death by inhalation, ingestion or by contact with skin. The most lethal form of exposure is inhalation of anthrax spores-bodies serving as vehicles for the bacterium. Alarmists say, "One billionth of a gram (of anthrax), smaller than a speck of dust can kill." But one anthrax spore, even thousands of spores, will not kill anyone.

Wool sorters inhale 150 to 700 anthrax spores per hour continually without danger. Laboratory studies indicate that about 10,000 spores are necessary to start an infection by inhalation. As with other toxins, it's the dose that makes the poison. Therein is the chief difficulty for anthrax as an effective mass terror weapon.

The technical hurdles and related expenses associated with exposing many people to enough anthrax is daunting. Aum Shinrikyo, the well-financed terrorist group that used nerve gas in the Tokyo subway in 1995, learned this lesson firsthand. The group employed scientists and invested a great deal of money in trying to develop anthrax into a weapon of mass destruction. The effort failed.

Anthrax spores are easy enough to obtain. But before spores can be made into a mass inhalation threat, they need to be converted to a powdered form. Liquefied anthrax would fall to the ground and be ineffective. In contrast to producing spores, "powder-izing" anthrax is no trivial task. Even assuming would-be terrorists had the technical know-how for producing mass quantities of powdered anthrax – without killing production workers and surrounding populations – the necessary facilities and development would cost hundreds of millions of dollars. Purchasing a few unemployed, ex-Soviet bio-weapons experts is not enough.

Not surprisingly, only the U.S. and Russia so far have succeeded in powder-izing anthrax for purposes of weaponry. Iraq is the most expected source of mass anthrax bio-terrorism. But Iraq only has anthrax in liquid form.

Even Iraq seems to know that its liquefied anthrax is virtually useless. United Nations inspectors found relatively few Iraqi warheads containing anthrax. Barring the idea that Iraq managed to sneak their anthrax stockpile out of the country shortly before the U.S. invasion, if Iraq had an effective form of anthrax, it would likely have been found in many more warheads – like the many Iraqi warheads containing nerve gas.

Iraq probably will never have anthrax capability. As Jane's Intelligence Review reported, "The Iraqis would have to maintain rigorous First World standards and not their usual 'make-do' efforts." Powder-izing anthrax is not the end of the challenge. Once released into the air, spores then become subject to atmospheric conditions. Too much wind will disperse spores into harmless concentrations. Not enough wind, the spores will fall to the ground and not arise again in harmful concentrations.

Airplanes dusting a city would be an unlikely choice for spreading anthrax spores. The few spores entering buildings would mostly settle; the few that didn't would likely be insufficient in concentration to cause infection. Outside, spores would likely fall to the ground or be blown away and rendered essentially harmless.

If enough spores were dropped, some people conceivably may inhale enough to become infected. But in the worst-case, this might happen to dozens, rather than thousands of people. An accidental release of anthrax spores at a Soviet bio-weapons laboratory in 1979 resulted in about 70 deaths in a metropolitan area of about one million people.

In reckless disregard for the prospects of mass anthrax terrorism, American Public Health Association executive director Mohammad Akhter wrote in the *Washington Post*, "A cloud of anthrax spores drifting over Arlington (Virginia) could kill tens of thousands of Washingtonians within days."

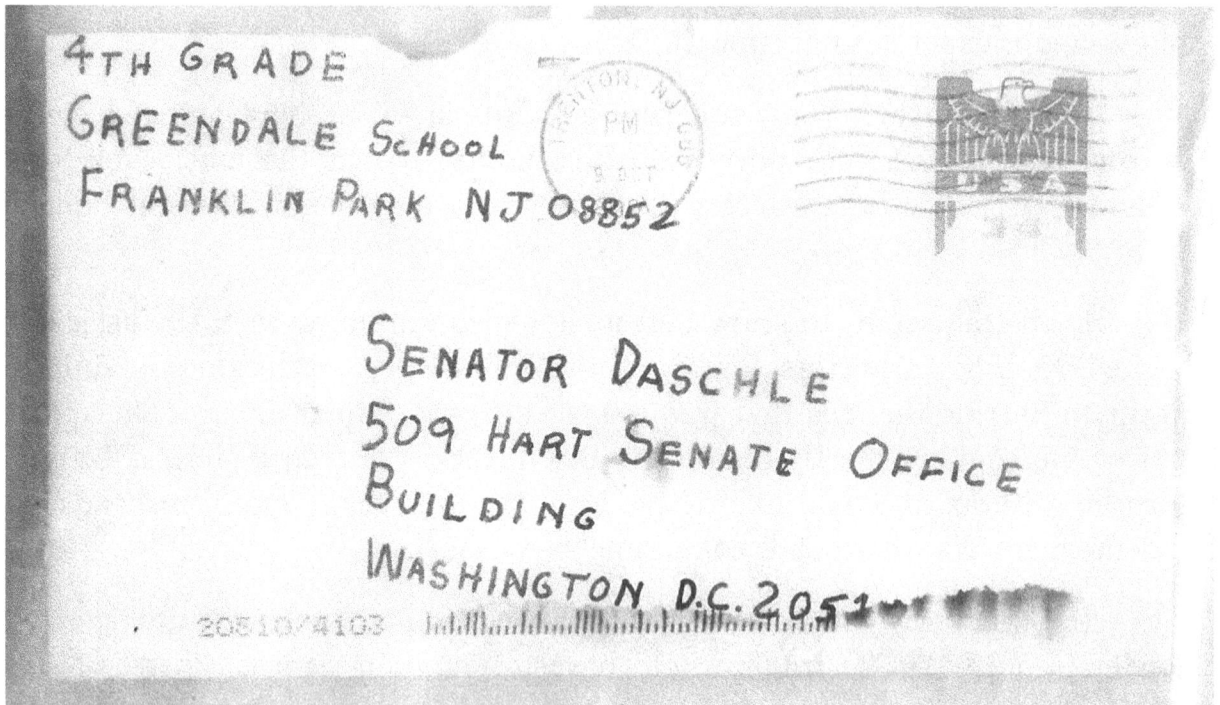

In September 2001, letters containing military-grade anthrax were mailed to several news media offices and two Democratic U.S. Senators. The anthrax spores ended up killing five people and infected 17 others. In 2005, Bruce Ivins, a scientist who worked at the government's biodefense labs at Fort Detrick, became a focus of investigation. After the FBI put Ivins under surveillance, he committed suicide in 2008. There is still doubt on whether or not Bruce Ivins was responsible for the anthrax terrorist attack.

CHAPTER NINE

A Conspiracy to Spread Disease and Death

ANTHRAX is just one of many diseases that could be potentially useful for dedicated terrorists. The British newspaper *The News Telegraph* has reported that the largest outbreak in history of a highly contagious disease that causes patients to bleed to death from every orifice was confirmed on Pakistan's frontier with Afghanistan. At least 100 people caught the disease and ten died. An isolation ward screened off by barbed wire was set up in the Pakistani city of Quetta.

"Evidence suggests the outbreak of Crimean-Congo Hemorrhagic Fever emanates from within Afghanistan, raising fears of an epidemic if millions of refugees flee across the frontier into Pakistan. CCHF has similar effects to the Ebola virus. Both viruses damage arteries, veins and other blood vessels and lead to the eventual collapse of major organs. As one doctor put it, a patient suffering from hemorrhagic fever 'literally melts in front of your eyes.'"

The location and the curious timing of this outbreak, the largest in history, raise serious questions about its origin. As Dr. Taj Mohammad of the Fatima Jinnah Chest and General Hospital in Quetta told a reporter: "It's unheard of...very unusual. There's a real risk of an epidemic among Afghan refugees."

A fact sheet distributed by the World Health Organization notes that, "Although primarily a zoonosis, sporadic cases and outbreaks of CCHF affecting humans do occur." The report goes on to say that, since the virus primarily affects animals, "The majority of cases (of human infection) have occurred in those involved with the livestock industry, such as agricultural workers, slaughterhouse workers and veterinarians."

There is no indication that the inordinately high numbers of Afghani victims were employed in such professions. How then did they contract this feared disease? Experts have speculated that the most likely culprit is "a species of tick, Hyalomma marginatum, and common in the [afflicted] areas." The WHO fact sheet notes that a "number of tick genera are capable of becoming infected with CCHF virus ..."

Is this outbreak then a natural occurrence? Not necessarily. A brief review of the use of insects as carriers of biological warfare agents is in order here. According to Robert Harris and Jeremy Paxman's book, *A Higher Form of Killing*, that history began during World War II when the Japanese "cultivated the plague-infected flea as a biological weapon. Pingfan [a bio-warfare lab] was said to be capable of producing 500 million fleas a year."

Following the war, that technology was warmly embraced by America's bio-warfare engineers, who had their Japanese counterparts flown over to the States to share the tricks of the trade. Fort Detrick, the longtime home of American biological warfare research, soon became the world's premier site for developing such weapons of war as the "flea bomb."

Among the potential agents studied at Camp Detrick were anthrax, glanders, brucellosis, tularemia, meliodosis, plague, typhus, psittacosis, yellow fever, encephalitis and various forms of rickettsial disease; fowl pest and tinder-pest were among the animal viruses studied; various rice, potato and cereal blights were also investigated.

Evidence clearly suggests that such weapons were used by the United States in the war waged against North Korea. American pilots captured during the war confessed while under torture to dropping flea bombs on the people of

North Korea, and Chinese officials published photographs of what they claimed to be "American biological bombs."

The U.S., of course, dismissed these reports as ludicrous, claiming that the pilots had been "brainwashed" into offering the confessions. The Chinese, though, assembled an international committee of scientists – from the United Kingdom, Italy, France, Sweden, Brazil and the Soviet Union – which in October of 1952 released a 700-page report that concluded that "the peoples of Korea and China did actually serve as targets for bacteriological weapons."

The detailed report listed the techniques that had been deployed in that war, "which ranged from fountain pens filled with infectious ink, to anthrax-laden feathers, and fleas, lice and mosquitoes carrying plague and yellow fever."

The U.S., needless to say, continued to deny and/or ignore the evidence indicating the use of bio-warfare agents. Along with other countries such as Russia, China and Iraq, the United States continued to research and develop these blatantly illegal and indiscriminate killers.

In 1956, the army began investigating the feasibility of breeding fifty million fleas a week, presumably to spread plague. By the end of the 1950s, the Fort Detrick laboratories were said to contain mosquitoes infected with yellow fever, malaria and dengue (an acute viral disease also known as Breakbone Fever for which there is no cure); fleas infected with plague; ticks contaminated with tularemia; and flies infected with cholera, anthrax and dysentery.

From 1950 through 1953, the U.S. Army released chemical clouds over six U.S. and Canadian cities. The tests were designed to test dispersal patterns of chemical weapons. Army records noted that the compounds used over Winnipeg, Canada, where there were numerous reports of respiratory illnesses, involved cadmium, a highly toxic chemical.

In 1951, the U.S. Army secretly contaminated the Norfolk Naval Supply Center in Virginia with infectious bacteria. One type was chosen because blacks were believed to be more susceptible than whites. A similar experiment was undertaken later that year at Washington, D.C.'s National Airport. The bacteria was later linked to food and blood poisoning and respiratory problems.

Savannah, Georgia, and Avon Park, Florida, were the targets of repeated Army bio-weapons experiments in 1956 and 1957. Army CBW researchers released millions of mosquitoes on the two towns in order to test the ability of insects to carry and deliver yellow fever and dengue fever. Hundreds of residents fell ill, suffering from fevers, respiratory distress, stillbirths, encephalitis and typhoid. Army researchers disguised themselves as public health workers in order to photograph and test the victims. Several deaths were reported.

In 1965, the U.S. Army and the Dow Chemical Company injected dioxin into 70 prisoners (most of them African-American) at the Holmesburg State Prison in Pennsylvania. The prisoners developed severe lesions which went untreated for seven months. A year later, the US Army set about the most ambitious chemical warfare operation in history.

From 1966 to 1972, the United States dumped more than 12 million gallons of Agent Orange (a dioxin-powered herbicide) over about 4.5 million acres of South Vietnam, Laos and Cambodia. The government of Vietnam estimated the civilian casualties from Agent Orange at more than 500,000. The legacy continues with high levels of birth defects in areas that were saturated with the chemical. Tens of thousands of U.S. soldiers were also the victims of Agent Orange.

In a still-classified experiment, the U.S. Army sprayed an unknown bacterial agent in the New York Subway system in 1966. It is not known if the test caused any illnesses. A year later, the CIA placed a chemical substance in the drinking water supply of the Food and Drug Administration headquarters in Washington, D.C. The test was designed to see if it was possible to poison drinking water with LSD or other incapacitating agents.

In 1969, Dr. D.M. McArtor, the deputy director for Research and Technology for the Department of Defense, asked Congress to appropriate $10 million for the development of a synthetic biological agent that would be resistant "'to the immunological and therapeutic processes upon which we depend to maintain our relative freedom from infectious disease."

It would appear then that the United States and other countries have a long history of researching and developing germs and infected insects as biological warfare agents and hasn't been shy about deploying such weapons specifically to inflict massive civilian casualties. Just one week before the

September 11 attacks, the *New York Times* reported that U.S. biological weapons research was still very much alive and well, though cloaked as always as defensive' research:

"Over the past several years, the United States has embarked on a program of secret research on biological weapons that some officials say tests the limits of the global treaty banning such weapons. The projects, which have not been previously disclosed, were begun under President Clinton and have been embraced by the Bush administration, which intends to expand them."

In 1971, the first documented cases of swine fever in the western hemisphere showed up in Cuba. A CIA agent later admitted that he had been instructed to deliver the virus to Cuban exiles in Panama, who carried the virus into Cuba in March of 1991. This astounding admission received scant attention in the press.

In 1981, Fidel Castro blamed an outbreak of dengue fever in Cuba on the CIA. The fever killed 188 people, including 88 children. In 1988, a Cuban exile leader named Eduardo Arocena admitted "bringing some germs" into Cuba in 1980. Four years later, an epidemic of dengue fever struck Managua, Nicaragua. Nearly 50,000 people came down with the fever and dozens died. This was the first outbreak of the disease in Nicaragua. It occurred at the height of the CIA's war against the Sandinista government and followed a series of low-level "reconnaissance" flights over the capital city.

In 1996, the Cuban government again accused the U.S. of engaging in "biological aggression." This time it involved an outbreak of thrips palmi, an insect that kills potato crops, palm trees and other vegetation. Thrips first showed up in Cuba on December 12, 1996, following low-level flights over the island by U.S. government spray planes. The U.S. was unable to quash a United Nations investigation of the incident.

At the close of the Gulf War, the U.S. Army exploded an Iraqi chemical weapons depot at Kamashiya. In 1996, the Department of Defense finally admitted that more than 20,000 U.S. troops were exposed to VX and sarin nerve agents as a result of the U.S. operation at Kamashiya. This and experimental vaccines may be the causes of Gulf War Illness.

The United States has already seen a case of germ-warfare conducted on innocent civilians. Due to the mass media's decision to ignore this incredible story, most citizens have no idea of the incredible events and conspiracies that took place in Oregon in 1984.

Bioterrorism of the Salad Bar

A religious cult known as the Rajneeshees, followers of Bhagwan Shree Rajneesh, a self-proclaimed guru exiled from India, had moved into a ranch in rural Wasco County, Oregon, took political control of the small nearby town of Antelope and changed its name to Rajneesh. Next, the cult sought to run the whole county by winning the local election in 1984.

The amazing story of the Wasco County election scandal was revealed by Leslie L. Zaitz, an investigative reporter for *The Oregonian*, and Dr. John Livengood, an epidemiologist at the Centers for Disease Control.

To win the county election, the Rajneeshees planned to sicken a good portion of the population in the town of The Dalles, where most Wasco County voters live. Their weapon of choice to keep local residents from voting was salmonella bacteria. Cult members decided to test the use of salmonella and, if successful, to contaminate the entire water system of The Dalles on Election Day. First, the Rajneeshees poisoned two visiting Wasco County commissioners on a hot day by plying them with refreshing drinks of cold water laced with salmonella. Then, on a shopping trip to The Dalles, cult members sprinkled salmonella on produce in grocery stores "just for fun." According to reporter Zaitz, that experiment didn't get the results they wanted, so the Rajneeshees proceeded to clandestinely sprinkle salmonella at the town's restaurant salad bars. Ten restaurants were hit and more than 700 people got sick.

"They apparently didn't expect it to be such a huge success," Zaitz said. "The attention attracted by the salad bar escapade brought hordes of health officials and investigators into The Dalles. It dashed the cult's plan to do worse on Election Day." Health officials soon pinned down salmonella as the cause of the sudden outbreak, but put the blame on food handlers. In 1984, who could have imagined bioterrorism?

The Rajneeshees also bused in and registered homeless people from all across the country so they could vote in the Wasco County '84 election. That plan failed when, alerted by the mass registration of the homeless, the state threatened to conduct administrative hearings on every new local voter.

The cult's conspiracy to contaminate the election failed and, a year later, the entire Rajneeshee commune collapsed under the weight of an internal conflict. Cult informers confessed to numerous crimes, including plots to kill the U.S. attorney, the state attorney general, and the guru's doctor, as well as the plot to contaminate the election. Vials of salmonella were found on the Rajneeshees' ranch. Zaitz and his investigative reporting team produced a twenty-part series on the Rajneeshees for *The Oregonian* starting in June 1985. After the commune collapsed, they went back and produced a follow-up series. Among other things, they learned that the Rajneeshees had secretly put together a top-ten hit list on which Zaitz's name appeared as number three.

"If anything, the local news media were restrained and conservative in their coverage of the salmonella episode," Zaitz said.

"There was nothing alarmist, nothing to trigger a public panic," he continued. "More aggressive coverage perhaps would have heated up already tense community relations with the commune. Yet the benign treatment also gave the Rajneeshees comfort that they could get away with it. Fortunately, the commune collapsed before that could happen. But consider this: If they knew reporters were watching closely, would they have even tried?"

Something like that might be said of the presidential balloting mess. If, in the days before the voting, reporters had focused on the botched job the nation's election districts were doing with voting procedures for the central political event of our democracy, the election of a president, would the balloting and ballot-counting have been quite so off-base?

For epidemiologist Livengood, however, who had been dispatched to Wasco County to solve the cause of the mysterious outbreak, the story had a different, simpler moral: "Don't eat at salad bars."

CHAPTER TEN

How Safe Is Our Food Supply?

EVEN when you see it from a jet, the sheer scale of farming in the heartland of North America is hard to comprehend. Each one of those squares or circles in the endless patchwork of maize and wheat, soy and alfalfa that rolls from horizon to horizon can measure a square mile-about 260 acres, the standard unit for field sizes in this part of the world. Farmers rarely stroll through fields that big. They might send in a sprayer every few weeks, and finally a harvester. Otherwise, plants on which millions depend for food are on their own.

Let's imagine, then, that from your plane you see a small cloud of something emitted from a pickup truck on one of the deserted access roads. You are the only person who saw it. No one notices that the crops have a new infection until harvest. Then the farmer may keep it quiet to protect the value of his crop, or perhaps the infection shows itself only when the crop is eaten, or when next year's seeds are planted. Choose your scenario.

Suppose it was a wheat field and the cloud was spores of a wheat smut. The fungus has little impact on the harvest because U.S. wheat is bred to resist it. But the disease is on the exclusion list of every wheat-importing country in the world. The U.S. loses a billion dollars in exports, there is economic ruin in the wheat belt, world grain prices rise and hunger and unrest stalk some Third World cities.

There again, perhaps it was a maize field, and the cloud was millions of whiteflies carrying a usually harmless maize virus that has been genetically engineered to make botulinum toxin. The toxin turns up in beer made partly with maize, and sickens some people. Next year, more maize is affected as local whiteflies acquire and spread the virus. Another food scare, another government's credibility in tatters. The U.S. launches a billion-dollar whitefly control program and burns thousands of acres of farm land.

Or it could have been a soya bean field, and the cloud was an aerosol of Pseudomonas tabaci – a bacterium that produces deadly tab toxin. Relatively few fields are affected, but soy is used throughout the food industry. The contaminated batch kills some cattle, then a few people. Too small an outbreak to count as a major threat to public health, but enough to fuel a massive food scare. U.S. soy bean exports grind to a halt. World fodder and meat prices skyrocket.

Improbable scare stories? That depends on who you ask. Crop bioterrorism may not have made it on to the agenda in Europe, but a growing band of plant pathologists and defense analysts in North America claim that if your aim is to wreak economic damage, destabilize governments, or simply get a business advantage, there are few easier targets than those lonely waves of grain.

No one is claiming that such attacks have already happened – although that has not been ruled out. But at a symposium on anti-crop bioweapons at the Joint American and Canadian Phytopathological Society meeting in Montreal, they argued that measures must be taken to stop bioterrorist strikes against crops becoming inevitable.

Crop diseases are not a new temptation. By the time the U.S. renounced bio-warfare in 1968, it had stockpiled 30,000 tons of wheat stem rust spores to drop on the Soviet Union and a ton of rice blast for Asia. The Soviet Union stockpiled wheat stem rust and pathogens of maize and rice. Iraq had a wheat smut bomb.

But what has changed is the objective of crop bio-warfare and the ease with which a "bio-bomb" might be deployed. The military motive has traditionally been to deprive an enemy of food during wartime, says Mark Wheel of the University of California at Davis, who studies bioweapons for the Federation of American Scientists in Washington D.C. This goal was so difficult to achieve, he says, that it helped convince the U.S. to abandon crop weapons research when it did. Terrorists, on the other hand, don't need to annihilate the whole harvest to disrupt trade or discredit authorities. If that's the goal, a little plant disease – or the rumor of it – goes a long way.

Even in rich countries, the average city has only enough food to last five days, writes Wallace Deen, a consultant formerly with the U.S. biological defense program, in a report published in the Annals of the *New York Academy of Sciences*. In poor countries, a slight reduction in harvest can raise staple food prices for the urban poor enough to spark civil disturbance. Witness Indonesia after the Asian financial crisis in late 1997 – relatively small price rises for rice fueled food riots in major cities around the country.

Health scares might be a better way to destabilize governments in the wealthy West. At the Montreal symposium, "everyone thought it significant that it only took a little bit of dioxin in Belgium to create a food scare, ruin the livestock industry, destroy food exports and bring down the government," says Norm Schaad, of the Foreign Disease and Weed Science Unit in Fort Detrick, Maryland, part of the U.S. Department of Agriculture (USDA). "A terrorist might do the same with only a small outbreak of the right crop disease."

Political or ideological enemies needn't be the only targets – rivals for export markets may also be tempting. China, a major corn exporter, would benefit if disease blighted U.S. corn, and vice versa. Even corporations could get in on the act. "Say one company grows pineapples in countries where production is limited by a pathogen, which does not occur in countries where a rival operates. The first company might even out this trade advantage by spreading the pathogen," says Wheel.

"The globalization of trade is the most important development for those who would use biological weapons against plants," says Deen. Bioterrorists can cause havoc, he says, by contaminating just a fraction of a crop. International trade restrictions will do the rest.

The Final Nail In Your Coffin!

Under the World Trade Organization's "phyto-sanitary" rules, a minor disease outbreak can take an entire crop off the export market. Take karnal bunt, a relatively mild – if highly infectious – wheat smut that turns grain black, sticky and inedible. When the smut blew into Arizona from Mexico, 32 countries, including China, banned U.S. wheat imports in one day. The U.S. spent hundreds of millions of dollars to eradicate the fungus and save its $5 billion annual wheat exports. This episode helped to fuel current U.S. fears of anti-crop weapons, as it dawned on plant pathologists that a deliberate attempt to sabotage U.S. grain exports might not look very different.

So much for motives, but what about means? Building a bio-bomb aimed at plants would be a far less ambitious undertaking than designing one to take out humans ("All Fall Down," *New Scientist*, May 11, 1996, p 32). A large-scale biological attack on people needs a carefully "weaponized" germ to ensure that pathogens normally spread by close physical contact can be transmitted through the air and still be infectious. Plant viruses, bacteria and fungi, on the other hand, are already adept at seeking out and destroying victims that don't move. They are conveniently adapted to be spread by the wind and insect vectors.

And although genetically engineered crop bioweapons may sound scary, there's little need for them. "You can always find a natural plant pathogen as nasty as anything you could create," says Anne Vidaver, head of the Center for Biotechnology at the University of Nebraska, Lincoln. One exception might be an otherwise benign virus engineered to produce a human toxin – harmless for the plant, but a nasty surprise for whoever eats it.

Naturally occurring fungi such as smuts and rusts are far more likely to be a crop bioterrorist's weapon of choice, says Vidaver. Fungal spores are tough and can infect crops in a wider range of growth stages and environmental conditions than most bacteria and viruses. Fungi can also produce potent toxins, so even a small infestation can make an entire harvest toxic.

Pathogens for plant bioterrorism are a lot less trouble to breed than those aimed at humans because they need not be highly specific to the target, or even destroy that much of a crop to have an impact. Just a small greenhouse full of the crop and a few pathogens collected from local crops – which are likely to be different from those to which the crops in your target country are immune – would   suffice. A plant biological weapon would even be safer to manufacture than one designed to attack humans, which can always turn on its creators.

All the same, preparing a crop bio-bomb would not be a trivial undertaking. For instance, the spores would have to be specially formulated to prevent dumping and to protect them from ultraviolet light. But with a little luck and a little technical expertise, a weapon could be cooked up in someone's backyard. They could even get away with it. Spray anthrax from a light aircraft over bustling Washington, D.C., and someone is going to notice. Spread spores of karnal bunt over the lonely plains of Kansas and in all likelihood nobody will see.

Agriculture may be the world's biggest industry, and the most vital for human well-being, but it is also one of the least secure. "You could do enough damage to achieve your goal just by bringing in a suitcase full of vials of the pathogen and strolling past a field with an atomizer," says Wheel.

What's more, natural outbreaks of novel plant diseases have multiplied dramatically over the past decade as food, seed and people cross borders at ever-increasing rates. In North America, 25 plant viruses alone are listed as new or re-emerging, while the European and Mediterranean Plant Protection Organization in Paris has an "alert list" of 31 fungi, bacteria and viruses that are threatening to invade Europe. "With all these novel infections happening naturally," says Vidaver, "it may not be obvious if an outbreak is deliberate."

One way to deter would-be bioterrorists is to deny them deniability. "If we could say where a pathogen comes from, we could narrow things down," says Schaad. To that end, his unit at the USDA has collected thousands of plant bacteria from around the world. The next step is to DNA fingerprint the bacteria so that when a suspicious outbreak occurs, plant pathologists will quickly be able to work out where the errant pathogen came from. There are no libraries for fungal and viral pathogens. "We spend millions collecting genetic varieties of crops, but nothing on collecting their pathogens," says Schaad.

In September 2000, then-President Bill Clinton announced that $215 million would be spent to upgrade a USDA agricultural quarantine laboratory on Plum Island off the coast of New York State to deal with threats to U.S. agriculture, including plant pathogens. The lab will be equipped to analyze pathogens sent in from any suspicious outbreak. Assuming, of course, that someone notices such an outbreak in the first place. Farmers are not obliged to notify the authorities when an outbreak occurs. An attack "could occur without us knowing it, because we really don't have the tools in place to detect it," says Floyd Hom, head of the USDA's research service.

"We need automated systems that will enable people to get immediate identification of pathogens in the field," says Schaad. Such systems would rely on DNA and protein analyses similar to those being developed to detect biological weapons aimed at people.

No amount of technology will help, of course, if there are not enough plant pathologists to police the crops. Even as the threat of natural and unnatural disease outbreaks increases, there is a declining number of people who can identify diseases in the field. Assuming you have identified a crop bioterrorist attack, how do you limit the damage? Fungicides can stop or slow the spread of a fungal disease. But for crops infected with bacteria or viruses, usually the only option is to burn them and eradicate any insect vectors, which can be extremely difficult and costly.

An alternative approach would be to rapidly replace contaminated crops with those that are resistant to the pathogen. Plant breeding companies are investing millions of dollars characterizing plant genes for food crops. In a few years, when a new disease strikes, it may well be possible to pull out the right resistance gene and breed it into the crop that is under attack.

The USDA has already identified 26 genes that protect against the barley stripe rust that was wiping out the crop in the northwest of the U.S. in 1995. But it takes resources and time to breed new characteristics into crops and get them out to the farms, so this line of defense will only be available to the wealthy West and at best can only reduce long-term damage. Consumer opposition to genetically modified crops could also make this approach uneconomical.

Nor is there any guarantee that there will always be a resistance gene available. Take wheat streak mosaic, a virus that is spreading in North America and can cause catastrophic crop losses. Despite extensive research, no one has ever found a resistant variety. Alternative strategies do exist – such as using genes from other species – but ultimately any attempt to engineer resistance into plants only works until bioterrorists find a new pathogen. With such strike and counter-strike, "the world could get itself into a bioweapons arms race," warns Brian Halweil of the Worldwatch Institute, an agricultural and environmental think tank in Washington, D.C.

According to Vidaver, the best strategy is to reduce the threat of crop bioterrorism in the first place. This goal, she says, can be achieved in part through limiting the spread of infections by abandoning the uniformity of modern farm fields in favor of diverse plant varieties and more crop rotation. Modern American farms, with their huge expanses of one variety of wheat, maize or alfalfa, are "a disaster waiting to happen," she warns.

With the ever-increasing threat of natural plant diseases, investing in improved vaccines and disease diagnosis and a move away from monocultures will actually give U.S. farmers more of an edge over its global competitors – even if the terrorists never strike.

CHAPTER ELEVEN

Nostradamus Predictions of World War Three

THE 16th century doctor and astrologer, Michel Nostradamus, is said to have made a number of accurate predictions concerning the early years of the twenty- first century. Literally hundreds of books have been written over the years attempting to accurately interpret his nebulous prophecies.

Interest in the Quatrains of Nostradamus was renewed after the September 11, 2001 terror attacks on New York and Washington, D.C. Many people sought information from books and websites about Nostradamus and whether he had made any predictions that could be accurate for the time-period.

Some modern interpretations of Nostradamus seem to indicate that we are poised on the brink of a third world war. The "big city" is burning and the "big war" that will last twenty-seven years may be references to the World Trade Center disaster and the United States subsequent bombing of Afghanistan. If Nostradamus could be so accurate with his predictions, what about our contemporary astrologers? Do they foresee the outbreak of the third world war? For once, most of them concur with each other. Though they agree that the times are disastrous, with "Mars, the planet of war and terrorism, being in association with Rahu and Ketu," they are still hopeful that the third world war may be averted.

One astrologer, who strongly differs, is popular Indian columnist Veenu Sandal. She opines that the seeds of the third world war could very well be present in the September 11ᵗʰ attack on America. "The planetary positioning today, according to Vedic astrology, is very much the same as it has been during all major conflicts in history – from the Mahabharata to the first and second world wars," she explains.

"The War will happen," says Veenu, "though this will not have disastrous consequences for India. In fact, India will emerge stronger and, by 2005, India should be a solid superpower, since it is already on an upward trend.

"During this War, curiously, China will come up as one of the major players, with America and Russia combining forces on the other side," she confidently predicts. "The war will of course affect the Middle East the most, and, though China will be the surprise element and the initial advantage will go to them, eventually America will overpower them. However, America may no longer be the supreme power it is today."

Astrologer Sunita Chhabra agrees that the present planetary positioning portends disaster. "Both the First World War and even Pearl Harbor happened under similar positions," she says. "The ascendant of the U.S. is Taurus and Mars is posited in Gemini, while Rahu and Ketu are passing over natal Mars. That's the reason for the U.S. troubles."

But the young astrologer strikes a hopeful note when she says, "The only thing that will probably save us from the third world war is that Jupiter is also positioned in Mars. The beneficiary rays from this planet can save the world from this disaster," she says.

Only time will show whether or not the world will once again plunge itself into madness and death. Nostradamus believed that his predictions could be avoided and disasters prevented. It is up to mankind to decide whether to continue forwards on the path of global destruction or to stop and heed the warnings of those who temporally pierced the veil of time to view the shadows of what is yet to come.

CHAPTER TWELVE

Aum Shinrikyo's Search for Tesla Technology

THE Japanese doomsday cult Aum Shinrikyo has already been mentioned in this book for their audacious subway attack using sarin gas. However, prior to this terrorist attack, Aum Shinrikyo had been actively pursuing knowledge of nuclear armaments, red mercury and, even more bizarrely, Tesla technology.

At its high point, Aum Shinrikyo had 40,000 followers in six countries and a worldwide network that brought it state-of-the-art lasers, lab equipment, and weaponry. Aum leaders targeted top Japanese universities, recruiting brilliant but alienated young scientists from chemistry, physics, and engineering departments. They forged relations with Japan's ruthless crime syndicates, the yakuza, and with veterans of the KGB and Russian and Japanese militaries.

The cult's leader, Shoko Asahara, taught his followers that there would be a worldwide apocalypse brought about by the U.S. attacking Japan with nuclear weapons. Asahara believed that he had been chosen to lead an army of "God's Chosen Ones" to defeat the U.S. in an "End of the World" battle.

However, before this could happen, Aum Shinrikyo needed weapons, advanced weapons, to defeat its enemies.

At Asahara's direction, the cult would use weapons of mass destruction (WMD) against Japanese society, thereby provoking a catastrophic social breakdown. Asahara was convinced that, amid the resulting death and confusion, Japan would blame the United States. Asahara would then step into the confusion and lead his followers to victory. With this master plan in mind, Asahara decided to invest very large amounts of Aum Shinrikyo's eventual $1 billion-plus financial empire into WMD research and development. The scope of Aum Shinrikyo's WMD research is wide and impressive. Not content with standard biological, chemical or nuclear work, the cult researched and invested in other, more exotic weapons offering the potential to inflict mass casualties. Aum Shinrikyo was determined to acquire any type of functional, even if non-traditional, WMD.

The trigger for the cult's shift from apocalypse survival to apocalypse initiation appears to have been its unsuccessful attempt to compete in Japan's 1990 parliamentary elections, on which it spent millions of dollars but garnered only a token number of votes.

The group's efforts to develop apocalypse-hastening weapons melded science and science fiction; members were fascinated by futuristic weapons concepts such as plasma guns that could atomize human bodies or mirrors several miles across that would float in space and reflect the sun's rays. Perhaps as a way to conduct this kind of off-the-wall experimentation, in 1993 the group purchased a large sheep station (ranch) in Western Australia, situated on the edge of the Great Victoria Desert in the community of Leonora.

It is now known that the New York chapter of Aum contacted the Tesla Society to gain access to Nikola Tesla's patents and designs. Also, Aum sent members of a Japan Tesla Society to the Tesla Museum in Belgrade to seek out his notebooks.

Tesla had theorized that the Earth is a massive electromagnet that ceaselessly creates power of unimaginable proportions. This latent power could be tapped without great technical difficulty to give humankind nearly unlimited power for peaceful uses or for the most diabolical warfare.

The Final Nail In Your Coffin!

Aum members reported that many of Tesla's most important papers were confiscated by the U.S. government and remain classified. As well, Tesla's name, practically unknown in Japan, is a household word to scientists of the former Soviet Union and Eastern Europe. Japanese scientists, in short, were being locked out of the 21st century.

The cult's sheep station in Australia (Banjawarn Station) was the scene of a bizarre event that has mystified scientists who were unable to offer a good explanation on what exactly happened.

On May 28, 1993, a large fireball was seen by several observers flying from south to north between Leonora and Laverton. This was immediately followed by a significant 3.9 Richter scale earthquake – picked up by 23 seismic receivers around Western Australia and the Northern Territory.

Many observers reported that the fireball, which was seen a little after 11:00 PM, passed overhead producing a pulsed roaring noise similar to a very loud road train diesel engine. After the seismic wave hit, they heard a huge, long, drawn out explosion.

The fireball was described as red in color with a very small, bluish-white conical tail. After it disappeared over the horizon, a near blinding, massive, high energy burst of blue-white light that lasted for about 3-5 seconds followed. This lit up the clear night sky as if it were daylight. Observers reported that they could see for miles in every direction at ground level.

A huge, red-colored flare was then seen to shoot high into the sky and this was immediately followed by a massive seismic ground wave that hit the observers nearest to "ground zero." The ground shook so violently that one person tending the camp fell over and rocks and beer cans rolled off of tables.

A loud blast then followed that was heard over a distance of 200 miles, minor quake damage was reported as far as 100 miles southeast of the "ground zero," the other directions (excepting Leonora to the southwest) being largely uninhabited. One engineer who was located that night in Laverton, with Gulf War experience of missiles and aircraft breaking the sound barrier, described it as "definitely a major explosive concussion wave blast (not a sonic boom) – similar to, but bigger than, a normal open pit mine blast."

A large deep red-orange colored hemisphere of opaque light with a silver outer shell lining then rose from ground level to hover around over the ground zero location. This structure, when fully developed, was approximately three times the size of a typical Goldfields setting Moon as seen by observers located 40 miles from it, and it "bobbed around a bit for nearly two hours before disappearing suddenly, as if someone threw the light switch off."

This "half soup plate structure" (looking like a "deep red, very large and half-set sun") was seen by two observers from widely separated locations, one at the Banjawarn station buildings and one at the Deleta station buildings.

Almost exactly one hour after the first big event, three observers (located at the Banjawarn station buildings) also saw a second, much smaller fireball, which appeared to rise from behind distant trees well south of the station perimeter and fly to the north in a high arc before coming down to ground level. This event created a second, but smaller, explosion and minor earthquake.

Even though the event was attributed to a falling meteor, no evidence on the ground was ever discovered. This is especially odd considering the eyewitness reports of a large explosion and seismic activity that had been recorded in Perth.

Many researchers have speculated that the blast was caused by the Aum cult testing a small nuclear device using red mercury procured from former Soviet sources. However, a lack of radioactive dust particles in Australian radiation laboratory dust collectors for that month seems to rule that particular scenario out.

Considering the interest the Aum cult had in Tesla technology, especially his experiments into "earthquake" type weapons, it is no wonder that investigators looked, and found, connections between the Aum cult and electromagnetic (EM) weapons being offered for sale by Russia.

Aum's interest in sophisticated earthquake, weather and plasma weapons was considered serious enough to launch a special investigation by the U.S. Senate Permanent Subcommittee on Investigations. Chaired by Senator Sam Nunn, the committee spent five months conducting hundreds of interviews of "both government and private individuals." These included classified briefings from numerous U.S. intelligence agencies. Their findings were published in October 1995 in a 100-page report on the Aum cult.

The Nunn report, in addition to outlining Aum's large international membership and massive finances of over U.S. $1 billion, (a lot of that money was also provided secretly by the Japanese government) also revealed the cult's fascination for Tesla weapons. The Senate report describes Aum's visits to the New York-based International Tesla Society (ITS), where they sought to obtain a number of his books, patents and papers.

A representative of the ITS told Senate investigators that Aum's interest focused on Tesla's experiments with "resonating frequencies" in connection with artificially "creating earthquakes." Significantly, the report also states that Tesla claimed "...with his technology he could 'split the world' in two."

This astonishing assertion closely parallels remarks made by Soviet Premier Krushchev to the Presidium in 1960, where he referred to "...the advent of a new class of Soviet Superweapon, so powerful it could wipe out all life on earth if unrestrainedly used." The comment, made at the height of the Cold War, clearly did not refer to nuclear weapons – already an integral component of the feared Soviet arsenal.

Not least, the Senate report mentions Tesla's development of a "ray gun in the 1930's, which was actually a particle beam accelerator," and which was said to be able to "shoot down an airplane at 200 miles." Following Tesla's death in 1943, the U.S. government seized his papers and research notes, placing them under national security lock and key.

In 1991, President Gorbachev and his aide and Politburo member, Alexander Yakovlev, offered the Japanese government the USSR's super-secret intercontinental range EM weapons technology – capable of producing earthquakes – for $900 million U.S. dollars. This EM weapons system had been on active service in the USSR since the early 1960s.

U.S. intelligence reports show that Japan had covertly purchased weapons from Russia using AUM members to make the transactions as cover for the Japanese government. This intelligence raises the possibility that a test site would be required for demonstrating the intercontinental range and effectiveness of said EM weapons system to the purchaser. The weapon would need to be "fired" from an existing KGB transmitter site somewhere inside Russia, and/or from a KGB-controlled naval vessel.

Obviously one or several test-firing demonstrations of the EM weapon system's capabilities would be in order before any money would be handed over for the weapon. What better way than to purchase an isolated Australian outback station to act as the independent Japanese target and test range? Practically no one lives in this desert to notice the tests. If someone did, they would obviously dismiss them as natural meteorites. And the biggest and most explosive test, and the one involving major earthquake initiation, was best conducted prior to the AUM's official residency there.

There are still a lot of questions left to be answered as to what exactly happened in the Australian outback in 1993. Did the Aum group, with the help of the Russian military and the Japanese government, actually secretly test an EM Tesla-type weapon? Or was it all just a coincidence that an earthquake would occur in exactly the same area where Aum bought land with money supplied by the Japanese government?

This fascinating part of top-secret history may end up largely forgotten unless further evidence is sought and uncovered. Perhaps it is hoped by those involved that it remains unquestioned and dismissed as just another crackpot "conspiracy theory."

**Original Caption: "Nikola Tesla holding in his hands balls of flame."
Tesla's accident in 1895 may have led to his later Dynamic Theory of
Gravity in which gravity is described as a "field effect." The presence
of highly charged, rotating magnetic fields could therefore influence
time/space within a localized area.**

Write for our free catalog of incredible books and other products you will not find anywhere else on the planet. Send your name and address to:

Global Communications
P.O. Box 753
New Brunswick, NJ 08903

Email: mrufo8@hotmail.com

www.conspiracyjournal.com

www.ingramcontent.com/pod-product-compliance
Lightning Source LLC
Chambersburg PA
CBHW081155270326
41930CB00014B/3160